A MOSTLY PEACEFUL BOOK

A REFUTATION OF THE LEFTISTS CULTURE THAT PLAGUED 2020

BY MICHAEL EDWARD MEBRUER

Published by Mindstir Media, LLC
45 Lafayette Rd | Suite 181| North Hampton, NH 03862 | USA
1.800.767.0531 | www.mindstirmedia.com

Printed in the United States of America

ISBN-13: 978-1-7367342-4-7

PROLOGUE

Let me start this book by saying, I am not an elite. I am not cultured, well-spoken, or Harvard-educated. Since the start of the COVID pandemic, I have been unemployed (my twenty-sixth birthday was not fun). For the last couple of years, I have lived with family in rural Louisiana. We live in a trailer, where one of the two bathrooms does not work. The one working bathroom is not in great condition. It takes the toilet fifteen minutes to refill after flushing. The shower usually only has enough hot water for about five minutes, and the sink does not give any hot water (this makes shaving my face difficult).

In terms of education, I went to public school for K-12. Most of my public school education comes from rural Kansas or rural Louisiana. I have a bachelor's degree in economics from LSU. But I did not start at LSU. I started at Baton Rouge Community College and transferred to LSU after two years, and I worked full-time for all four years of my schooling.

When I say I am not cultured, it is not a lie. My favorite foods are Southern foods such as boiled crawfish, fried boudin balls, and red beans and rice. My favorite time of the year is when the NFL season starts. Although, I do like the NFL better when players keep their politics out of it.

The point I am trying to make is that there is nothing special about me. I am not wealthy; I am certainly not an elitist. But I know what I am, and that is a proud American.

I want to make one thing clear so that there is no misunderstanding. I adamantly oppose racism and white supremacy. Despite this, I am certain that I will be labeled "racist" or a "white supremacist," but I feel that it is worth mentioning that racism is one of the stupidest ideas that mankind has ever had. It has ruined many people's lives, destroyed the possibility of countless friendships, and has divided this country for many years. There is so much more to a person's story than the color of his or her skin. It does not matter whether you are white, black, brown, or yellow; we all bleed red.

I wanted to write this book because I have seen the Left steamroll through the culture in 2020. I have seen the Left defend rioting and looting by calling these events "mostly peaceful protests." A good example is when a CNN chyron called one riot, "Fiery But Mostly Peaceful Protests After Police Shooting." The chyron was on the screen while the reporter was in front of fires started by "mostly peaceful protesters."

The mostly peaceful line is what inspired the title of this book. It did not make sense. If these protests were peaceful, why did citizens board up their windows? Why were people scared? It turns out they were not peaceful. It was just an attempt by the media to cover for certain political organizations (something they would not have done for any sort of right-wing protest). This "mostly peaceful" logic is a joke. By this logic, the *Titanic* was a mostly successful voyage. For the majority of the time, the ship was above water. Everything was fine. All you have to do is forget the part where the ship hit the iceberg and sank. The final flight of the *Hindenburg* was a mostly successful voyage. It flew for over two hundred hours without incident. At the end of the day, can you really say that a couple of minutes can define whether or not something is a disaster?

I guess American statues were mostly unvandalized. In all seriousness, I saw American statues and monuments being toppled and vandalized. At first, it was Confederate statues that were being torn down. It is worth noting that I do not support Confederate statues, but I did not agree with how these statues were being taken down. I feel that those statues should be taken down safely by the city and put into a museum. With a plan like that, no one risks injury and the history behind the statue can be preserved. But then the mobs started vandalizing statues of Ulysses S. Grant and demanding statues of Abraham Lincoln be removed.

I saw white people kneeling to black people and begging for forgiveness. I saw this and could not believe that Americans would actually kneel to other people. I always felt that the idea of America is that we are a free people, and we do not submit ourselves to the will of others. I thought we stopped kneeling to men and kings over two hundred years ago.

I saw Chick-fil-A CEO Dan Cathy suggest that white people should shine black people's shoes, which seems kind of weird to me. If some random stranger came up to me and just started shining my shoes, my reaction would be something like, "Who the hell are you? Get away from my feet, you weirdo!"

Then I saw photos of white people washing the feet of black people. There were also strange group rallies in which people appeared to pray and ask forgiveness for white privilege. That is kind of funny because aside from worshipping the gender-neutral gods of global warming, I always figured the Left to be unreligious. Yet, they seemed to act in a religious manner.

Good men that fought racism like Lincoln and Grant were being torn from our history. I felt that no matter what, the culture would look at my conservative values and see racism. I felt that I would have to treat blacks unequally by my standards to treat them "equally" by someone else's standards. I felt that America was losing itself, and I had to be quiet and watch it happen.

To top it off, America was dealing with a cancel culture, an idea that falsely claims it is about kindness or decency. What truly drives cancel culture is forceful conformity. People could not have opinions without the risk of losing their jobs. Newspapers could not publish opinion pieces by certain politicians without backlash. Comedy and entertainment were becoming dull and boring.

This cancel culture reminded me of an episode from the *Twilight Zone*. The episode is named "The Eye of the Beholder." This brilliantly edited episode is about a woman who is considered so ugly by society that she risks being exiled with others like her if a cosmetic surgery does not make her beautiful. Throughout the episode, the doctors' faces are hidden due to a lack of light, and the woman's face is always bandaged. When the doctors remove the woman's bandages to see if the surgery was a success, the doctors gasp at how ugly the woman is. The surgery had failed. However, when the audience is able to see the woman, she is actually beautiful. When the doctors turn the lights on, they reveal themselves to be ugly. As the woman makes a futile attempt to escape, a dictator is shouting in a propaganda video. One of the things that he states is that there should be "a single norm, a single approach, a single virtue, a single morality." And that "we should cut out all that is different like a cancerous growth ... It is essential in this society that we not only have a norm but that we conform to that norm! ... Conformity we must worship and hold sacred!"

Well, I have never been one to allow others to tell me how to live my life. This book is an act of defiance against the leftists, conformity, and their cancel culture.

"Follow the path of the unsafe, independent thinker. Expose your ideas to the dangers of controversy. Speak your mind and fear less the label of 'crack-pot' than the stigma of conformity. And on issues that seem important to you, stand up and be counted at any cost."

THOMAS J. WATSON

PART 1

INTRODUCTION

CHAPTER 1

AN INTRODUCTION TO LEFTISM

First, it is important to define a leftist. An American leftist and an American liberal are not the same. Both believe in higher taxes and more government. However, liberals tend to favor the American systems, freedom, and view race as insignificant when judging someone. Liberals were the original people to say, "I might not like or agree with what you say, but I will fight tooth and nail for your right to say it." Examples can include people like John F. Kennedy and Martin Luther King, Jr.

A leftist will usually follow a post-modernist mindset; a leftist will view American systems as oppressive. Leftists do not believe in freedoms, such as freedom of speech, because they look at these freedoms as systems of power that are used to oppress others. Because they see freedoms as oppressive, they do not value them. For Example, leftists are quick to call any speech they do not like hate speech. When leftists hear speech that they do not agree with, they will say something like, "I might not like or agree with what you say, so you should not speak."

When it comes to race, leftists adopt identity politics. This is the idea that you will group yourself with others according to factors such as race, gender, and sexual preference. Leftists create a hierarchy of victimhood, which can then determine the value of someone's opinion. For example, a homosexual will be higher in the hierarchy than someone who is straight, or someone who is black will be higher in the hierarchy than whites. So, someone at the top of the hierarchy is probably a homosexual black transgender woman. At the bottom is the evil straight white cisgender male.

Leftists try to use identity politics as a form of anti-racism. Ironically, identity politics is used by white supremacists. Like leftists, white supremacists believe that race is very important and that a person's worth can be determined by someone's skin color. Both believe that group identity is more important than the identity of the individual. And people should act according to their group identity.

Leftist attempts at anti-racism can promote the same talking points that white supremacists use. In July of 2020, The National Museum of African American History and Culture released a chart that essentially promoted white supremacy.[26] The chart credited the following to white people: objective and rational linear thinking, hard work, self-reliance, and many more things. How is this chart any different from white supremacists, who claim blacks are lazy and irrational? It's not. And it shows the Left's bigotry of low expectations.

For starters, it gives the sense of black inferiority. It's racist and inaccurate to suggest that only white people have the

ability to work hard or have self-reliance. I don't know what the logic is behind this. What do leftists think blacks did in Africa for thousands of years? Blacks are no different than any other group of people. They had to hunt, farm, fish, gather supplies, and provide for their families. If someone were too lazy or incompetent to find food, their families would starve. Someone in Africa may have faced different climates and wildlife, but that does not mean that they did not have to work hard or

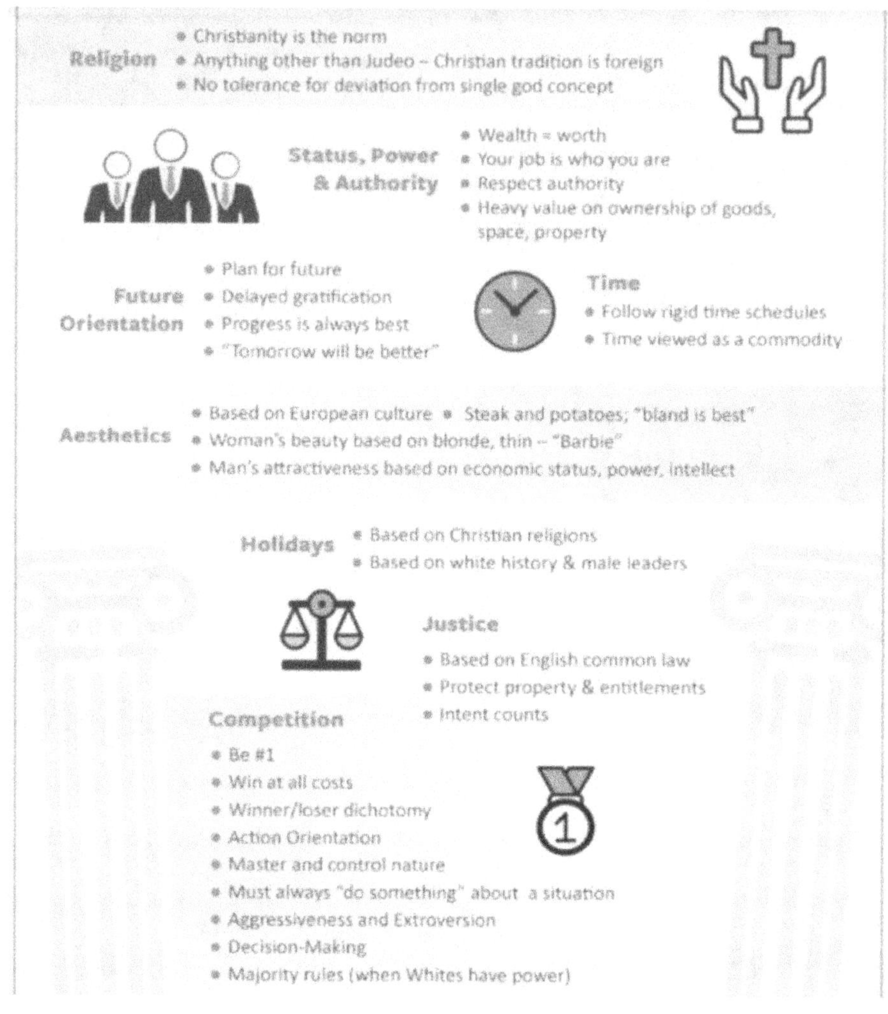

think critically in stressful situations. People across all cultures had to adapt to harsh situations. People had to innovate new farming, hunting, or gathering methods. When something went wrong, people had to change what they were doing or risk certain death. "Evolve or die," as they say.

Another problem with this is that it suggests that blacks should not have these traits, despite being essential for success. Some of the traits that stand out the most are hard work, self-reliance, and delayed gratification. These leftists will suggest that blacks should not work hard or engage in self-improvement. But what happens when blacks follow this advice and stop engaging in these behaviors? They fail. They fall into poverty, and any gaps between blacks and whites will likely increase. And the whole-time leftists will blame the "Racist American System," suggesting that blacks have no chance of success in the United States because of the bad outcome blacks will face. So, this idea of "black identity" ultimately becomes a self-fulfilling prophecy for black failure.

Something interesting is how a leftist will view a conservative. When leftists view me (a conservative white man), the leftist will have a love-hate relationship. On the outside, they will scream, shout, and show all kinds of anger toward me. Why? Because I have a different opinion of the world than they do. I champion the ideas of individualism, freedom, and personal responsibility; I do not view groups of people as victims. I consider it a victory in civil rights when there is equal opportunity, not equal outcome. This is the opposite of the identity politics approach commonly used by leftists. If we are opposites, then why do they love me as well? Well, a leftist does not love me. The leftist loves that there is someone out there who supports American systems that lead to disparities among groups. Because I am "privileged," it means that (according to leftists) I am trying to uphold systems of racism (or patriarchy if you are arguing with modern feminists). This allows for leftists to confirm their belief that white supremacy is running wild, even though my reasons for supporting American systems have nothing to do with race. They hate me because I am different from them, but they need me because they believe I confirm their worldview.

I mentioned above that a straight white cisgender male is at the bottom of the leftist hierarchy. The fact that I am conservative adds another layer of hate from leftists. Despite this, there is someone that leftists hate even more than white conservatives: black conservatives. Leftists have a hate-hate relationship with black conservatives. You see, a leftist will hate the ideals of a conservative, regardless of race. But, when a black person says, "I am not a victim" or "I can do this on my own," this shatters the leftists' view. This is because leftists are trained to see blacks as victims. But when the "victims" tell the leftists that they disagree with them and do not need leftists to speak for them, this creates conflict. This is problematic because the leftists' tactics that are used on whites do not work on blacks. For example, a white leftist would be quick to tell me to "check my privilege." But a white leftist can't say that to a black person because leftists consider white people more privileged than blacks. The checking of the privilege goes up the privilege hierarchy, not down. And so, the leftist is forced to deal with someone who disagrees with them, contradicts their ideals, and is immune to the identity politics approach. Despite this, leftists have found a way to deal with black conservatives. The leftists try to claim that the black conservative is not really black. The leftists claim that black conservatives that do not think or act a certain way are traitors against "real black people." Black conservatives are then labeled as an Uncle Tom or some other derogatory term. There is no diversity of thought in the "real black community."

Just ask the most articulate man in 2020, Joe Biden. The presidential candidate and possible future president said the following, "What you all know, but most people don't know. Unlike the African American community, with notable exceptions, the Latino community is an incredibly diverse community with incredibly different attitudes about different things." During the campaign, Biden also said, "Well I tell you what, if you have a problem figuring out whether you're for me or Trump, then you ain't black." Breaking everything down to a single factor leads to leftists oversimplifying and mischaracterizing problems whether it is on the campaign trail or anywhere else.

HOW A LEFTIST SEES PROBLEMS

always disliked how a leftist perceives a problem. It reminds me of an old *Saturday Night Live* sketch. In the sketch, Melissa McCarthy plays Barb Kellner, a woman who wants to get a small business loan for her pizza business. The problem is that her business involves people paying her for eating pizza. When asked how she came up with the idea, Kellner responds, "I was familiar with and read the book, *Do What You Love and the Money Will Follow*. And I said, 'Barb ... you love eating pizza.' So, we're gonna make like two, three, a couple million dollars eating pizza." The idea seemed crazy to the loan manager. The manager asked Kellner what part of the book she read. Kellner responded, "Well, I thought, 'Whoa, what a title!' I thought that said it all. So, I just closed that book and put it back on the shelf." Shockingly, Barb "the Pizza Eater" Kellner did not get her loan.

It may sound crazy, but some people on the Left see things that way. They will look at a basic statistic, note a discrepancy, assume discrimination, and then close the book and put it back on the shelf. This can apply to issues of race, gender, sexual preference, etc. An example of this is the "gender wage gap." US Census Bureau earnings data from 2018 showed a considerable difference between the median income for men and women. For leftists, this was proof that women were being oppressed in the workplace because the median white woman was making seventy-nine cents for every dollar the median white man made.[29]

But this study barely even scratched the surface. It did not control for factors such as work experience, levels of education, hours worked, or even the occupation. The proper way to prove a bias would be to control for these factors. For example, you can compare the salary of a female registered nurse with less than one year of experience working in New Orleans to that of a male registered nurse with similar experience and education who is also working in New Orleans. If you control for these factors and there is still a significant difference, you can argue for the gender wage gap. But you must be able to control for as many of the contributing variables as possible. In other words, you have to read more than just the title of the book to understand it.

I believe that systemic blaming involves more creative thinking than analytical thinking. These people find a stat or disparity that they do not like, and they craft a narrative that fits the disparity. When someone who is more analytical sees something they do not like, it simply opens the door for more investigation. The analytical person then tries to see the entire picture. The creative approach is easier. It is not hard at all; I can do it too.

For example, did you know that the first three *Jurassic Park* movies are feminist films that secretly promote female violence against men? For starters, all the problems that occur in the films are due to men. The reason the dinosaurs are made is because of John Hammond, the CEO of INGEN. This is a dog whistle for how short-sighted men are. The dinosaurs get out because of Dennis Nedry, the head of Jurassic Park systems. He shuts down the park's systems so he can commit corporate espionage. Nedry gets what he needs, but he also gets eaten by dinosaurs. This is a dog whistle saying that men are greedy and incompetent and are the cause of all problems. The women are superior to the men and often save the day. In the first *Jurassic Park*, teenager Lex Murphy is the one that gets the system back online and saves the day when no man could. That is not the only time women are portrayed as superior. In the first *Jurassic Park*, game warden Robert Muldoon is killed by raptors. It does not matter that Muldoon was a skilled hunter, armed with a shotgun, and knew the raptors could coordinate attacks. The raptors were just too clever. Compare this to the second *Jurassic Park* movie. Kelly Malcolm, a teenage girl, beats the raptors with gymnastics. Seriously. She used a pipe to do flips and kick a raptor out of a window. The raptor falls on some spikes and gets impaled. And the best part is that she got cut from her local gymnastics team. So, a teenage girl who does gymnastics is more capable of surviving raptors than an armed and experienced hunter? Are you starting to see the matriarchy? If not, I have even more evidence. All the deaths that occur in the first three *Jurassic Park* movies are male deaths. And it is not like there was a lack of death. Twenty-six males died in the first three *Jurassic Park* movies. I suppose that it is only fitting that all the dinosaurs on the islands are female. Obviously, *Jurassic Park* movies have a distaste for men and show that women have all the power.

Okay, I'll stop there before #CancelJP starts trending. No, I do not think that *Jurassic Park* is sexist towards men. The point I am trying to make is that it is not hard for people to make these huge leaps in logic to match two things together. The difference is that I did this with a movie. Leftists apply this way of thinking to real-world problems. It is why they assume that any disparity means discrimination, and every conservative is a white supremacist.

CHAPTER 3

OPPONENTS OF LEFTISM

There are many opponents to leftism. Contrary to what leftists may say, they come in a large variety of people. Some people who oppose leftism are white, others are black, and some are Jewish. That is just the superficial diversity. There is a great deal of intellectual diversity among people who oppose leftism. There are conservatives, liberals, moderates, teachers, musicians, psychologists, authors, writers, comedians, MMA fighters. These people have different experiences and beliefs. What unites them is the belief everyone should be able to add their ideas to the marketplace of ideas.

As I noted before, leftists tend to disagree with this philosophy. Leftists believe that any who oppose leftism are committing some sort of violence against leftists. How do leftists respond? With violence. And that is not code for intellectual debates. Leftists will physically assault, harass, and threaten violence against people that they disagree with. Here are three examples of how the Left has treated opponents of leftism.

Daryl Davis

Daryl Davis is a black American author, musician, and activist. He is also the author of *Klan-destine Relationships: A Black Man's Odyssey in the Ku Klux Klan*. In a Joe Rogan Experience interview,[2] Davis revealed that he deradicalized around two hundred white supremacists, and convinced the white supremacists to leave the KKK and other hate groups without even asking anyone to leave. Davis simply showed the former white supremacists that as a black man, he was not who the KKK had falsely portrayed him to be.

What separates Daryl from most activists against white supremacy is that he attended KKK rallies. It sounds crazy, right? A black man attending a KKK rally sounds like a sheep attending a party for wolves. The story gets even crazier. Mr. Davis was invited to the rallies by his friend Roger Kelly, an Imperial Wizard of the KKK.

In his *TEDx Talk*,[1] Davis says that he met Roger Kelly when Davis was working on his book. Davis wanted to understand why racist people thought that way. He figured the best source for understanding racism could come from a national leader in the KKK. The interview lasted for a couple of hours, and Davis arranged for more meetings with Kelly, even allowing these meetings to happen at Davis's house. Eventually, these meetings turned into an unlikely friendship. This friendship continued as the years passed. Eventually, Kelly invited Davis to Klan rallies. Davis would attend the KKK rallies, and Kelly would watch Davis's band perform. The two continued to be friends and grow a mutual respect. In the interview with Joe Rogan,[2] Davis noted that as the friendship continued, what Davis and Kelly had in common would outshine how they were different (skin color). After about six or seven years, Kelly left the KKK and gave Davis his old robe. Due to his friendship with Davis, Kelly did not believe in the message the KKK stood for anymore.

Davis has a theory on where hate comes from. He believes it all starts with ignorance. As he said in his TEDx video, "Ignorance breeds fear, we fear things we do not understand. If we do not keep that fear in check, then fear in turn will breed hatred because we hate those things that frighten us. If we do not keep that hatred in check, that hatred, in turn, will breed destruction." Davis continues, saying that one of the things needed to beat this ignorance is respect. "Respect is the key. Sitting down and talking, not necessarily agreeing, but respecting each other to air their points of view."

This is nearly the opposite of how leftist groups deal with those they disagree with. The leftist playbook consists of trying to tear down the opposition's platform. This involves getting speeches and events canceled. Daryl Davis was no exception.[3,4] In 2019, Davis attended an event called "Ending Racism." Antifa took offense to this platform that wanted to create an open dialog for people across the political spectrum. Antifa threatened to burn down the theater the event was being held at. Some members even called Davis a white supremacist. It seems insane that people would call a man who has been so impactful in the fight against white supremacy a racist. However, it just shows the ignorance of the people who were protesting this event. And if there is any truth to what Davis has said, the hatred from the Antifa comes from its ignorance, the same ignorance that causes white supremacists to hate others that do not think as they do.

Ben Shapiro

Ben Shapiro is a conservative American political commentator, author, and editor-in-chief of *The Daily Wire*. He partners with the Young America's Foundation to give speeches on college campuses. His speeches cover topics from identity politics, current political events, and other conservative values.

Shapiro gave a speech at UC Berkley in 2016, and the event went as planned. However, things were more complicated when Shapiro went to give another speech at UC Berkley in 2017. This time Shapiro was accused of being a fascist, white supremacist, and a friend of the Alt-right. It may seem absurd to consider Ben Shapiro an ally to anti-Semitic white supremacists. But the people who said these things probably did not know anything about Ben Shapiro. Shapiro is an Orthodox Jew and has openly denounced groups like the Alt-right. In an interview with ABC, Shapiro said, "I've been very outspoken against the Alt-right. I've said the Alt-right is a garbage movement with garbage ideas. That it has nothing to do with constitutional conservatism."[6]

He was met by far-Left activists who wanted to shut down the event. Some of the protesters threatened the event with violence. Others were content to disrupt or cancel the event. One of the leaders of this group told ABC that Shapiro should not be able to speak. The leader did not care about Shapiro's right to speak and that the First Amendment of the Constitution was not a relevant document.[6]

The speech lasted about thirty minutes. Shapiro talked about fascism, identity politics, personal responsibility, and individual freedom. He also made it a point to thank local law enforcement and condemn the identity politics of the far-Left and the Alt-right. While Shapiro was able to speak and answer questions, there was a cost to the event. Berkley spent $600,000 on extra security, and eight people were arrested.[5]

The incident at Berkley is not the only time Shapiro has been accused of being associated with the Alt-right. In 2019, *The Economist* wrote an article about Shapiro. The title was, "Inside the mind of Ben Shapiro, the Alt-right sage without the rage."[8] After large online backlash, the title of the article was changed to, "Inside the mind of Ben Shapiro, a radical conservative." This is a prime example of the Left conflating conservatism with white supremacy. Not only has Shapiro spoken out against the Alt-right, but he has been one of their biggest targets for harassment. Anyone with an ounce of journalistic ability (or integrity) could have found Shapiro's feelings towards the Alt-right. But I guess it is easier to call an Orthodox Jew a Nazi.

Drew Brees

If there is one person on this list that is not like the others, it is Drew Brees. Drew Brees is not known as a political commentator who speaks out against the dangers of political correctness. He is a future Hall of Fame quarterback for the New Orleans Saints.

As a fan of the Tampa Bay Buccaneers, Brees has been a major thorn in my side for years. In June of 2020, Brees seemed to anger everyone over "controversial and insensitive statements." From the way everyone reacted, it seemed like Drew Brees said something awful. These comments could have ranged from: "I worship Satan," or "I am friends with Richard Spencer," or even "I plan to vote for Donald Trump." What did Drew Brees say that was so bad? When asked about players kneeling during the national anthem, Brees said the following:

I will never agree with anybody disrespecting the flag of the United States of America or our country. Let me just tell you what I see or what I feel when the national anthem is played and when I look at the flag of the United States. I envision my two grandfathers, who fought for this country during World War II, one in the Army and one in the Marine Corps. Both risked their lives to protect our country and to try to make our country and this world a better place. So, every time I stand with my hand over my heart, looking at that flag and singing the national anthem, that's what I think about. And in many cases, that brings me to tears, thinking about all that has been sacrificed. Not just those in the military, but for that matter, those throughout the civil rights movements of the '6os, and all that has been endured by so many people up until this point. And is everything right with our country right now? No, it is not. We still have a long way to go. But I think what you do by standing there and showing respect to the flag with your hand over your heart is it shows unity. It shows that we are all in this together; we can all do better and that we are all part of the solution.[20]

Aren't his statements utterly repulsive? The audacity to show a basic love for one's country. Note that Brees was not condemning the people that kneeled for the national anthem. He did not try to get them fired or "canceled." He simply stated that he disagreed with the people who kneeled for the anthem and explained why he stands for it.

But this is America. We can just agree to disagree, right? Wrong. Drew Brees was out of line with the ideals of leftism.

So, it was time to summon the outrage mob, which included LeBron James, Michael Thomas, and many more. Saints safety Malcolm Jenkins gave a response video. Jenkins cried as he said:

> It shows you don't know history because when our grandfathers fought for this country and served and they came back, they didn't come back to a hero's welcome. They came back and got attacked for wearing their uniforms. They came back to racism and complete violence ... The same brothers you break the huddle down with before every single game, the same brothers you bleed with and go into battle with every single day, go home to communities that have been decimated ... Unfortunately, you're somebody who doesn't understand his privilege. You don't understand the potential you have to actually be an advocate for people call brothers ...[56]

There are three problems I have with this video. First, Malcolm Jenkins was crying. This is a problem because Malcolm Jenkins is what I like to call "a grown-ass man," and a man should not be crying just because someone gave an opinion that he does not like. Second, Jenkins said that Brees is someone who does not understand his privilege. It is worth noting that Malcolm Jenkins signed a $32-million contract paid over four years with the Saints (at least $16 million is guaranteed). A multi-millionaire acting like he is not living a life of privilege—his lack of awareness is amazing. Lastly, Jenkins says that teammates of Brees go back to decimated communities. A rookie drafted in the seventh round will make over $600,000 a year. The NFL minimum salary paid to players is $480,000. So, it is safe to assume that anyone who plays in the NFL will be in the top 5% of income earners in the US I highly doubt that these wealthy athletes are living in high-crime, low-income areas.

However, facing the backlash, Brees apologized. Saying in part:

> I would like to apologize to my friends, teammates, the City of New Orleans, the black community, NFL community, and anyone I hurt with my comments yesterday. In speaking with some of you, it breaks my heart to know the pain I have caused. In an attempt to talk about respect, unity, and solidarity centered around the American flag and the national anthem, I made comments that were insensitive and completely missed the mark on the issues we are facing right now as a country.[22] See note for full apology statement.

I was terribly upset that Brees apologized. I can relate to what Drew Brees said in his original statement. Like Drew Brees, I have family that served in the military. My father served in the Marines. My great-grandfather served in the Navy during World War II. Men like them kept this country safe and its people free. I love my country, and I am a proud American, despite everything America has done in its history. One of the greatest freedoms is that you can say what you want in this country. It is unfortunate that someone who loves his country must apologize. No one should ever be ashamed to be an American. America is truly a great and wonderful place that offers more freedom than anywhere else.

I know that loving America is not popular with leftists. In fact, hatred for America and its history is the driving force behind one of the most popular movements in 2020—the Black Lives Matter movement.

BLACK LIVES MATTER

WHAT IS BLACK LIVES MATTER?

Black Lives Matter was founded in 2013, following the acquittal of George Zimmerman for the death of Treyvon Martin. Black Lives Matter is an activist movement that targets systemic oppression and seeks social justice. Below are many of the talking points, goals, and objectives Black Lives Matter has supported or called for.

"Our members organize and build local power to intervene in violence inflicted on Black communities by the state and vigilantes. Black Lives Matter is an ideological and political intervention in a world where Black lives are systematically and intentionally targeted for demise. It is an affirmation of Black folks' humanity, our contributions to this society, and our resilience in the face of deadly oppression." [10]

Some of the other beliefs that Black Lives Matter include: [10]

"We acknowledge, respect, and celebrate differences and commonalities."

"We work vigorously for freedom and justice for Black people and, by extension, all people."

"We disrupt the Western-prescribed nuclear family structure requirement by supporting each other as extended families and 'villages' that collectively care for one another, especially our children, to the degree that mothers, parents, and children are comfortable."

"We are self-reflexive and do the work required to dismantle cisgender privilege and uplift Black trans folk, especially Black trans women who continue to be disproportionately impacted by trans-antagonistic violence."

"We are guided by the fact that all Black lives matter, regardless of actual or perceived sexual identity, gender identity, gender expression, economic status, ability, disability, religious beliefs or disbeliefs, immigration status, or location."

The following are a couple of mission statements for different chapters.[10]

Black Lives Matter Chicago Chapter- "Black Lives Matter Chicago is an intersectional vehicle that values Black people and our right to self-determination. We fight for justice with families most impacted, while working to create just and equitable systems. We work to end state violence and criminalization of Black communities by deconstructing white supremacist, capitalist patriarchy."

Black Lives Matter Boston- "Black Lives Matter Boston remains committed to being active in the Movement for Black Lives (M4BL), and its broad mission platform. BLM Boston centers work against racist policing and police violence, abolishing mass incarceration, economic disparities, and factors that allow the school-to-prison pipeline to exist.

"WHO WE ARE

Point #1 — BLM Boston galvanizes our communities to end state-sanctioned violence against Black people.

Point #2 — BLM Boston supports the development of new Black leaders, as well as create a network where Black people feel empowered to determine our destinies in our communities.

Point #3 — BLM Boston follows a queer Black feminist theory of creating change within the Black communities."

Black Lives Matter Washington DC- "We are a radical collective of Black artists, infrastructure-builders, movement-healers and strategists from the future, organizing in the here and now. Black Lives Matter DC is a member-based abolitionist organization centering on Black people most at risk for state violence in DC, creating the conditions for Black Liberation through the abolition of systems and institutions of white supremacy, capitalism, patriarchy, and colonialism.

"We are dedicated to promoting strategies that:

— empower the most oppressed Black people.

— do not reinforce or legitimize systems and institutions that harm Black people, including police, prisons, mass incarceration, and modern slavery.

— divest from people, institutions and systems that harm us and invest in the people, institutions, systems and other models that support our liberation and empowerment.

— use a diversity of tactics to promote harm reduction, political education, and non-cooperation as strategic visions."

Black Lives Matter became more popular after the death of Michael Brown. On August 9, 2014, in Ferguson, Missouri, an unarmed eighteen-year-old black male named Michael Brown was shot by white police officer Darren Wilson. There was a wide variety of speculation. Reports were suggesting that Michael Brown had been shot in the back. Others reported that Michael Brown had his hands up and said, "Don't shoot" before being shot. This acted as the catalyst for the Black Lives Matter movement. Black Lives Matter organized protests in Ferguson. "Darnell Moore and Patrisse Cullors organized a national ride during Labor Day weekend that year. We called it the Black Lives Matters Ride. In 15 days, we developed a plan of action to head to the occupied territory to support our brothers and sisters. Over 600 people gathered."[10]

One of the biggest policies that Black Lives Matter has suggested in 2020 is to defund the police. In a video,[9] Black Lives Matter made a claim that "more than 1000 men, women, and children are killed by police in the United States every single year, and thousands more are brutalized and abused. The police are out of control." Black Lives Matter furthers their argument by saying that police reforms do not work and "That's why everyone is saying it's time to defund the police … Defunding the police is the only way to stop pouring resources into a system that does not make us safe." The video ends with the idea that less money should be spent on police and more money should be invested in the black community. These investments include teachers, counselors, mental health and restorative services, and community-led harm reduction.

CHAPTER 2

FALSE CATALYSTS

I use the term "false catalyst" in this chapter to explain the effects high-profile deaths at the hands of police had on Black Lives Matter. I use the term "catalyst" because Black Lives Matter has had several high-profile cases over the last couple of years that helped the organization grow. These cases could have acted as a catalyst for BLM in multiple ways that can range from increased public support or opinion, more recognition for the organization, and even its founding (remember that BLM was founded after the death of Treyvon Martin).

I describe these catalysts as false because they are built on false narratives. Understandably, there may be some misconceptions or misinterpretations when an incident first occurs. But journalists and law enforcement investigate the claim and find more information over time. You would expect there to be more public knowledge and clarity for the facts of each case. Unfortunately, this does not happen. Misinformation and false narratives continue to be spread by irresponsible politicians and media figures. For this chapter, I will focus on two cases that led to large-scale support and growth for Black Lives Matter—the case of Michael Brown, who was killed in 2014, and George Floyd, who was killed in 2020.

Michael Brown

Michael Brown was shot by Officer Darren Wilson on August 9, 2014. Brown was unarmed at the time of the shooting. This led to the narrative that an unarmed innocent black man had been shot by police. The media also pushed stories that stated that Brown had been shot with his hands up. There were other stories of people saying that Brown had been shot in the back. Some stories were combined, suggesting that Brown had been shot in the back while his hands were raised and was trying to surrender. This acted as one of the biggest catalysts for the Black Lives Matter movement. And that catalyst is built on a lie. Barack Obama's Department of Justice launched an investigation into this shooting. Most of the information in this section is based on that investigation.[19]

For starters, Brown was not innocent. Moments before the shooting, Brown committed unarmed robbery from a local convenience store. According to the report, "Brown stole several packages of cigarillos. As captured on the store's surveillance video, when the store clerk tried to stop Brown, Brown used his physical size to stand over him and forcefully shove him away. As a result, an FPD dispatch call went out over the police radio for a 'stealing in progress.'" Wilson suspected that Brown and his friend were involved in the robbery when he saw them because they matched the suspects' description and were carrying cigarillos.

The report also states that Brown assaulted Wilson while Wilson was in his police vehicle. Brown tried to take Wilson's gun, and Wilson fired his weapon in self-defense. Autopsies on

Brown suggests that Brown's hand was inches from the muzzle of Wilson's gun. A bullet was also recovered from inside the SUV's driver side door.

Brown then tried to flee, and Wilson pursued Brown, fearing that Brown could be a danger to himself or others. According to the report, "the autopsy results confirm that Wilson did not shoot Brown in the back as he was running away because there were no entrance wounds to Brown's back." This disproves the claim that Brown had been shot in the back.

Several witnesses said that Wilson shot Brown because Brown began to charge at Wilson. This suggests that Wilson was justified in his use of force because Wilson was defending himself. These witness statements also disprove the claim that Michael Brown had surrendered and said, "Don't shoot."

"Witness 102 told investigators that he knew "for sure that [Brown's] hands were not above his head." Rather, Brown made some type of movement similar to pulling his pants up or a shoulder shrug, and then "charged" at Wilson ... According to Witness 102, crowds of people had begun to gather, wrongly claiming the police shot Brown for no reason and that he had his hands up in surrender ... all of Witness 102's statements were materially consistent with each other, with physical and forensic evidence, and with other credible witness accounts."

"According to Witness 111, at no time were Brown's hands up in surrender or otherwise."

"Other witnesses who have suggested that Brown was shot with his hands up in surrender have either recanted their statements, such as Witnesses 119 and 125, provided inconsistent statements, such as Witness 124, or have provided accounts that are verifiably untrue, such as Witnesses 121, 139, and 132."

Other witnesses agreed that Brown's shooting was justified and sided with Officer Wilson. However, they did not wish to speak, due to fear from community or media backlash.

"Witness 108 is a 74-year-old black male who claimed to have witnessed the shooting, stated that it was justified, but repeatedly refused to give formal statements to law enforcement for fear of reprisal should the Canfield Drive neighborhood find out that his account corroborated Wilson."

"Witness 109 is a 53-year-old black male. Like Witness 108, Witness 109 claimed to have witnessed the shooting, stated that it was justified, and repeatedly refused to give formal statements to law enforcement for fear of reprisal should the Canfield Drive neighborhood find out that his account corroborated Wilson."

"Witness 113 is a 31-year-old black female. She was interviewed one time by FBI agents during their canvass on August 16, 2014, and gave an account that generally corroborated Wilson, but only after she was confronted with untruthful statements she initially made in an effort to avoid neighborhood backlash. When local authorities tried to serve Witness 113 with a subpoena to testify before the county grand jury, she blockaded her door with a couch to avoid service ... She explained to the FBI that, "You've gotta live the life to know it," and stated that she feared offering an account contrary to the narrative reported by the media that Brown held his hands up in surrender."

In a sub-note on page 83 of the report, it was noted, "The media has widely reported that there is witness testimony that Brown said "don't shoot" as he held his hands above his head. In fact, our investigation did not reveal any eyewitness who stated that Brown said, 'don't shoot.'"

Despite this investigation, there are still people that claim that Michael Brown was murdered. This can be due to several things, but I would say the biggest one is the media. I remember when the media covered this. They did not pull any punches. Furthermore, they seemed more or less complacent in stoking racial tensions and pushing false narratives. After the investigation by the DOJ, I do not remember any mainstream media outlets recanting their statements. It's as if the media went along with this narrative, and when the facts did not support their claims, they went completely silent. This was not the only time this happened.

George Floyd

George Floyd is a case that should be fresh in everyone's memory. George Floyd died while in police custody on May 25, 2020. This case gained so much attention early on because of a cell phone video that caught Floyd on camera. In this video, Floyd was handcuffed, laying on his stomach, and police officer Derek Chauvin had his knee on the back of the neck of George Floyd. Floyd is distressed and is pleading with police officers, saying, "I can't breathe," multiple times. George Floyd died later that day.

I would say the entire country was outraged by what we saw. This was nothing like the Michael Brown case. This was the police acting in a barbaric and brutal manner, slowly extinguishing the life of a fellow American citizen.

Even cop-loving, rural conservatives such as my family and I were appalled by this. I remember when the video first started making the news. My conservative aunt saw the video and said, "They should be ashamed of what they did to that poor man." I agreed. I believed that there was no question of whether

Derek Chauvin should be sent to prison. The only question was whether it was for murder or manslaughter.

This was a great boon for BLM. At the start of 2020, BLM had the support of around 42%[98]. Around that same time, opposition to BLM was around 32%, and the people who neither supported nor opposed BLM was around 24%. The death of George Floyd caused support for BLM to spike. Following the death of George Floyd, support went from 45% to 52% … in a week.

But why do I have George Floyd in this chapter? His killing was not justified because he was not a danger to the police. And I supported the prosecution of Derek Chauvin before. What changed? New information and context about the incident.

For starters, it is entirely possible that the knee to the back of the neck did not kill George Floyd. Or at least it was not the primary cause of death. The medical examiner of Hennepin County performed an autopsy on George Floyd. When talking about the neck, the report says the following:

"Neck: Layer by layer dissection of the anterior strap muscles of the neck discloses no areas of contusion or hemorrhage within the musculature. The thyroid cartilage and hyoid bone are intact. The larynx is lined by intact mucosa. The thyroid is symmetric and red-brown, without cystic or nodular change. The tongue is free of bite marks, hemorrhage, or other injuries. The cervical spinal column is palpably stable and free of hemorrhage."[99]

So, what did kill George Floyd? It is possible that he experienced an overdose on fentanyl. The autopsy showed that Floyd had a serum fentanyl level of 11 ng/ml in his system at the time of death. As we all know, fentanyl is very potent and can be lethal even in small doses. A study by Academic Emergency

Medicine showed the effects of several patients experiencing fentanyl.[100] One patient had a serum fentanyl level of 7.9 ng/ml, and he had to be administered Naloxone (a medicine used to counteract the effects of fentanyl). To my knowledge, George Floyd had not been administered Naloxone. It is entirely possible that the fentanyl was a primary contributor to Floyd's death.

This leads to other evidence and context that was later released. There is a full video of the police officers' body cameras,[102] as well as the transcript[101] of the encounter with Floyd. Floyd appears to be distressed throughout the video. His behavior is not violent, but it is erratic. When Officer Lane first encounters Floyd at Floyd's vehicle, he has to tell Floyd multiple times to keep his hand where Lane can see them. Floyd does not comply. Officer Lane finally says at one point with his weapon drawn, "Put your hand up there. Put your fucking hand up there! Jesus Christ, keep your fucking hands on the wheel." When Lane tries to get Floyd out of the vehicle, Floyd pleads with Lane not to shoot him. Lane responds with, "I'm not shooting you, man." When cops try to put handcuffs on Floyd, he does not cooperate at first. He does not act aggressively towards the police, but he resists the cops putting the handcuffs on him. When Floyd walks with the police, he falls down several times. It probably was not intentional; it may have been due to his distress.

Police then take George Floyd to the patrol car and attempt to put him in the back seat. George Floyd pleads and yells at the police officers not to put him in the car. Floyd says on multiple occasions that he is claustrophobic. Floyd asks the officers if they will crack the window for him. Officer Lane says, "Yes, I'll crack it. I will."

Floyd was still reluctant to get in the car. For over a minute and a half, police actively tried to get George Floyd into the car. Floyd did not let the cops put him in the car, yelling and panicking the entire time. During this part, a bystander yells, "Bro, you about to have a heart attack and shit. Man, get in the car!"

During this struggle, Floyd starts to yell, "I can't breathe!" and requests to be laid on the ground. The police officers decide to stop trying to put him in the car and put him on the ground. Once the cops get Floyd on the ground, Floyd starts panicking there as well. And it is about that time where the cell phone video that everyone saw begins.

This video shows a lot of things that people did not know before. It shows that Floyd failed to cooperate with the police on multiple occasions. It showed that he was distressed and erratic. It showed that police did not want to put Floyd on the ground. They tried on multiple occasions to put Floyd in the back of the police car. And lastly, it shows that Floyd was having issues breathing before Chauvin put his knee to Floyd's neck. Floyd was saying he could not breathe when officers were trying to put him in the car.

Do I think Floyd's death is a tragedy? Yes, I do. But Floyd's death is not the murder that BLM and the media painted it to be. I do not think either of the two recanted their statements about it. They pushed the narrative for as long as possible, and when new evidence came out, they stopped talking about it.

Having to spread lies and misinformation is not the right way to spread your ideology. I have always believed that if you must lie to others to get them to join your cause, maybe your cause is not a good one. It is because of this, the core of BLM is wrong.

CHAPTER 3

THE CORE OF BLACK LIVES MATTER IS WRONG

As I start this chapter, I would like to note a disingenuous tactic used by Black Lives Matter activists. BLM activists will try to get people to say, "Black lives matter." The problem is that the phrase "black lives matter" has multiple meanings now. If I say, "Black lives matter," am I saying that I believe that there is value in a black person's life? Or am I expressing support for an anti-police Marxist movement that wants to disrupt the nuclear family? When asked the question, "Do you think black lives matter?" a common response is, "Yes, black lives matter because all lives matter." This response is intended to acknowledge that there is value in black lives without supporting the BLM organization. But the BLM supporter will say, "So you don't think black lives matter," which implies that the other person is a racist. This creates a false dichotomy fallacy because it implies that there is no middle ground on the issue. But the truth is that people can value black lives and not support an organization like BLM. When it comes to black lives matter, I believe the words are true, but the movement is a lie.

The core belief of Black Lives Matter is that Black Americans are "systematically and intentionally targeted for demise." I argue that this is false and that there is no statistical evidence to support this claim.

As mentioned in the previous chapter, Black Lives Matter says, "more than 1000 men, women, and children are killed by police in the United States every single year ..." This is true. In 2019, 1017 people were killed by the police. What Black Lives Matter does not tell you is that out of all the people killed, 250 people (25%) were black. 403 people (40%) were white, 162 people (16%) were Hispanic, 41 people (4%) were listed as "other race," and 143 people (14%) are listed as an "unknown race."[12]

Of the 250 Black Americans shot by police, only 14 (5.6% of total blacks shot) were unarmed. Out of all the police shootings, only 1.4% were committed on an unarmed black person. It is also worth noting that of the 403 white people shot by police, 25 were unarmed. This means that 6.2% of whites killed by police were unarmed. This shows that the rate of unarmed deaths (5.6% for blacks and 6.2% for whites) are nearly even.[12]

Being a police officer is not a safe or easy job because police interact with people who are on drugs or have a mental illness. Sometimes, a suspect is violent, and police officers must defend themselves. Police will usually try non-lethal methods in these encounters. But there are cases when police officers have to defend themselves from dangerous suspects. In most police shootings, the suspect is armed, or the police officer faces high or significant threat levels.[11] Even in cases when the suspect is unarmed, he can still pose a significant danger to police. Sometimes these dangers result in police officers dying in the line of duty. According to the FBI, in 2019, 48 police officers were feloniously killed in the US and Puerto Rico (2 killed in Puerto Rico). Out of the 48 police officers killed, 44 were killed by a suspect with a firearm. The other four officers died from vehicles being used as a weapon.

Below is a brief chart the tells the name and threat levels of unarmed black people killed in 2019.

Name	Date of Incident	Threat Level
1. Michael Dean	12-02-2019	Undetermined (Officer Carmen Decruz charged with manslaughter)[15]
2. Christopher Whitfield	10-14-2019	Undetermined
3. Atatiana Jefferson	10-12-2019	Other (Officer Aaron Dean charged with murder)[16]
4. Melvin Watkins	09-16-2019	Undetermined
5. Channara Tom Pheap	08-26-2019	Attack
6. Josef Delon Richardson	07-25-2019	Undetermined
7. Ryan Twyman	06-06-2019	Other
8. Kevin Pudlik	06-03-2019	Other
9. Isaiah Lewis	04-29-2019	Attack
10. Marcus Mavae	04-11-2019	Attack
11. Marzeus Scott	04-07-2019	Attack
12. Kevin Bruce Mason	03-24-2019	Other
13. Gregory Griffin	01-28-2019	Other (Officer Johnny Crespo charged with manslaughter)[17]
14. Jimmy Atchison	01-22-2019	Undetermined

Table is due to reference 11 and 12

"As described in the story, the general criteria for the attack label was that there was the most direct and immediate threat to life. That would include incidents where officers or others were shot at, threatened with a gun, attacked with other weapons or physical force, etc. The attack category is meant to flag the highest level of threat. The other and undetermined categories represent all remaining cases. Other includes many incidents where officers or others faced significant threats."[14]

One argument that I have heard is "blacks account for 25% of the deaths from police, but only make up 13% of the US population." The logic in this argument is flawed and based on random probability. There are two more important variables: the number of police interactions and the violence of the criminal.

One reason why the "blacks account for 25% of the deaths from police but only make up 13% of the US population" argument does not work is because interactions with the police are not based on random probability. For example, a cop does not stop every twentieth car he sees and give the driver a ticket. The police officer will observe a driver that is speeding or not wearing a seatbelt. Then he will pull the car over and give the driver a ticket. Encounters with law enforcement are dependent on criminal activity. That is why crime rates are a better dependent variable than population. If a group has more encounters with the police (arrests), there will be an increased chance for an incident. By 2018 FBI statistics,[18] of the total arrests in the United States, 27.4% were black. This rate is nearly the same as the 25% rate of police shootings.

The other variable in the chances of a police shooting is how violent the criminals are during the police encounters. Like I said before, most people who are shot by the police pose a significant threat to the officer's life, and violent criminals are more likely to pose a threat to police officers. The FBI defines violent crime as "offenses of murder and nonnegligent manslaughter, rape, robbery, and aggravated assault."[18] Of the individual violent crime rates in 2018, blacks committed 53.3% of murder and nonnegligent manslaughter, 28.6% of rapes, 54.2% of robberies, and 33.7% of the aggravated assaults. In total, blacks committed 37.4% of violent crime. The fact that the violent crime rate is so high in the black community can explain why the percentage of blacks being shot by police is not proportional to the black population of the US.

Black Lives Matter claim that there is a systemic targeting of blacks for demise, usually by the state or white supremacists. The data does not support this claim. For starters, there are no systematic killings of blacks by the state. Over 40 million blacks are living in the United States. Two hundred fifty black deaths at the hands of police officers (most of them were justified shootings) does not indicate that there is a system designed to have blacks murdered by the police.

So, police are not systematically targeting black Americans. What about white supremacists? While they do engage in disgusting acts of terrorism, white supremacists are not causing a systemic killing of blacks. From the beginning of 2015 to the end of 2018, white supremacists and Neo-Nazis killed 48 people. White supremacists killed 36 people in this timeframe. Neo-Nazis killed 12.[65] (Note: The Global Terrorism Database does not distinguish victims by race, but not all victims were black. For example, the Santa Fe school shooting by a Neo-Nazi on May 18, 2018.)

Blacks are more likely to be killed by other blacks. In 2018, 2925 black or African Americans were murdered (and the victim's case was solved). Of the 2925 homicides, 2600 of the murderers were black, 234 murderers were white, and the other 91 homicides were committed by either an unknown or other race.[13] This information shows that other blacks committed 88.8% of black homicides. It is worth noting that most white murders (80%) were committed by other whites. Therefore, most murders committed in the United States are done intra-racially.

CHAPTER 4

POLICIES SUGGESTED

Black Lives Matter has considered several different policies. These policies range from the disruption of the nuclear family to defunding the police. I will first discuss what BLM activists have considered when it comes to defunding the police. There have been several different variations of defunding the police. Some groups have called for a reduction in police resources. Others have gone as far as demanding the disbanding of entire police forces. For argument purposes, I will use the recommendation in Chapter 1, which involves decreasing the resources of the police.

Black Lives Matter plans to defund the police in three steps.

- **First.** Demand that lawmakers support reparations for all families of those killed by police violence.
- **Second.** Demand that every state, city, and municipality spend less on law enforcement and incarceration. Period.
- **Finally.** Demand investment into black communities. It is not enough to defund the police; we need to put in

place systems to uplift and protect black communities. That means divesting from (police in schools, criminalizing mental health, military weapons against citizens) and investing in (teachers and counselors, mental health and restorative services, and community-led harm reduction.)"[103]

For the first step, these laws already exist. Families can sue the city in instances of wrongful death. An example is Philando Castile. For those unfamiliar with the case, Philando Castile was stopped for a broken taillight in July 2016. Castile informed Officer Jeronimo Yanez that he was carrying a firearm. At one point, Yanez believed he saw Castile reaching for his firearm and shot and killed Castile. While Officer Jeronimo Yanez was acquitted of manslaughter, Castile's family filed a wrongful death suit against the city. The city of St. Anthony settled and paid the Castile family three million dollars.

The idea behind the second step is to decrease the police resources so there can be fewer cops on the streets. Black Lives Matter must assume that fewer cops on the streets will make communities safer. Unfortunately, this is far from reality.

For starters, the anti-cop rhetoric coming from Black Lives Matter and the media can discourage, demoralize, and negatively affect the ability of law enforcement. It can cause what Heather Mac Donald calls the "Ferguson effect."[30] The Ferguson effect can be defined as cops disengaging from discretionary enforcement activity and the 'criminal element feeling empowered.' In *The War On Cops,*[30] Mac Donald says, "With police so discouraged, violent crime has surged in dozens of American cities ... Homicides were up 76 percent in Milwaukee, 60 percent in St. Louis, and 56 percent in Baltimore for the year (2015) through mid-August, compared with the same period in 2014. Murder rates were up 47 percent in Minneapolis and 36 percent in Houston through mid-July."

New York City saw its own "Ferguson effect" in June of 2020. It did not help that on June 15, the NYPD disbanded an anti-crime unit of 600 officers. In June 2020, New York City saw large increases in certain crimes when compared to June 2019.[33] Murder in NYC increased 30% (from 30 in 2019 to 39 in 2020). Burglary increased by 118% (817 in 2019 to 1783 in 2020), and shooting incidents increased by 130% (89 in 2019 to 205 in 2020).

Black community leaders wanted the cops to return, noting the increase in crime. "The African American community is saying we don't want crime here. Ninety-five percent of the people here are decent, law-abiding citizens, and the law is for the lawless," Bishop Gerald Seabrooks told reporters Tuesday following a spate of five shootings early Monday night in Canarsie. "So, please, mayor, take your handcuffs off of the police. Let them police with professionalism, respect, and courtesy."[34]

The last part of the plan, involving divesting from (police in schools, criminalizing mental health, military weapons against citizens) and investing in (teachers and counselors, mental health and restorative services, and community-led harm reduction), is flawed.

There are parts in the divesting portion that do not make sense. For starters, police officers do not patrol the streets with military-grade weapons. A police officer will have a handgun that can vary based on the police departments. Police officers also use pepper spray, knives (uncommon and are mostly used to cut ropes or seatbelts), police batons, and a taser. A cop car will have a shotgun in case the officer needs it, and the officer can choose between lethal (buckshot) and non-lethal (beanbag rounds) ammunition.[35] Most of a police officer's weapons are non-lethal (or at least have a non-lethal component) and are designed for close range. This does not compare to the lethality of an army standard-issue M4 rifle or a Claymore mine. An M4 rifle is designed for automatic and semi-automatic firing. The M4 can fire almost 1000 rounds per minute and be precise and deadly for up to 500 meters. The Claymore mine contains 700 metal balls and 1.5 pounds of C-4 explosive within it; the Claymore has the capacity to kill anything within fifty meters of it. If you compare the killing potential of police equipment to actual military equipment, it is foolish to consider police equipment military-grade.

Divesting from the criminalization of mental health does not make sense either. Having a mental illness is not a crime. Cops are not arresting people for depression. If they were, Millennials would be in trouble. Society tries to be accommodating for people with mental health issues. For example, it is illegal for firms to discriminate based on mental health. According to the US Equal Employment Opportunity Commission, Americans are provided protections under the Americans with Disabilities Act (ADA) "If you have depression, post-traumatic stress disorder (PTSD), or another mental health condition, you are protected against discrimination and harassment at work because of your condition, you have workplace privacy rights, and you may have a legal right to get reasonable accommodations that can help you perform and keep your job."[36] If a mentally ill person commits a crime, they are arrested for breaking the law and not for having a mental illness.

Getting police officers out of schools and hiring more teachers and counselors will not be productive. Police officers in schools are there to keep the students safe and maintain order in the school. Officers are mostly used as a deterrent to threats both inside and outside the schools. As I previously noted, decreasing police presence in vulnerable communities leads to higher crime. If cops are removed from high-crime areas, how long before the violence moves into the schools? And if police officers are no longer in schools, do you expect teachers to stop acts of violence? Kerstin Westcott resigned from her teaching position at a Green Bay public middle school due to the chaos in the school. Westcott said that both students and teachers were terrorized by students in the school. "I fear for my safety every day. I am equally afraid for my colleagues and, most importantly, my students. We are in danger every day when we show up to our school … We exhibit symptoms of PTSD (post-traumatic stress disorder) because we live in trauma from 07:30 to 3:00 every single day."[37,38] The school had police officers at the school, but they were restricted to the cafeteria because that's where a lot of the fights were. If there were no police officers in schools like these, the schools would descend into anarchy. And this school was not that far from anarchy. Westcott noted that truant students would roam the hallways looking for fights. Westcott had to lock the doors to keep those students from coming into her class and assaulting her students. With unsafe environments like this, it would not matter how much money you offered teachers; many would refuse the job out of fear for personal safety. Schools need to be safe for both teachers and students, and it is unfair and impractical to put the burden of maintaining order on teachers.

The BLM Chicago Chapter engaged in a campaign to defund the police. The chapter wanted to stop the building of a police training center in Chicago. They referred to this as #NoCopAcademy. This goes hand in hand with the idea that giving police officers fewer resources and less funding will be beneficial. The problem with this line of thinking is that it can deny police departments the resources needed to have better-trained police officers. What happens if cutting police resources reduces the quality of police officers? If police officers are not properly trained to deal with stressful situations, it can lead to more unnecessary deaths (an example of an unnecessary death can be the Castile case). Stopping the building of the police academy lessens Chicago's access to better-trained police officers. Also, police need funding for body cameras and dashboard cameras. I believe that it is important to hold police accountable for their actions. These cameras can give important information about encounters police have with their community.

A useful way to think of police is to think of them as most goods or services. A good or service can have three characteristics: high quality (well trained and equipped officers), have high quantity (a large number of officers), and low cost (small police budget). Police departments can have two of these characteristics at one time but never all three. For example, A police department can have high quality but low quantity. This leads to a police department that is well trained but has fewer police officers, which means that the police department does not need as much funding. Theoretically, this can work for small towns or rural areas, but if this is tried in large cities like Chicago or NYC, police departments will be overwhelmed. No police department should try a low quality, high quantity approach. Police departments may end up with a cheaper police department, but you will have a high number of poorly trained and equipped police officers. That is a disaster waiting to happen. The potential disasters can be several things. One potential disaster is a higher number of police deaths. If police are not as well trained to deal with dangerous situations, there may be an increase in police casualties. Another disaster is that there could be an increase in wrongful deaths at the hands of police. If police are not properly trained to deal with stressful situations, they may respond poorly in these circumstances. The best combination for large cities is to have high quality and high quantity police forces and accept the costs that come with it.

Another harmful plan Black Lives Matter has is to bring the end of the nuclear family. "We disrupt the Western-prescribed nuclear family structure requirement by supporting each other as extended families and "villages" that collectively care for one another, especially our children, to the degree that mothers, parents, and children are comfortable."

For starters, this has almost been accomplished. The percentage of non-marital births has increased in the black community. The percentage of non-marital births for blacks was 38% in 1970. It increased to 67% in 1990 and was at 71% in 2014. In 1970, 35% of black children lived with a single parent. In 2014 54% of black children lived with a single parent. The marriage rate has declined in the black community. The marriage rate for blacks in 1970 was 60%. In 2014 it was 35%. These trends are not exclusive to the black community. In the white community, non-marital births increased from 6% in 1970 to 29% in 2014. In 1970, 10% of white children lived with a single parent. It was 19% in 2014. The marriage rate for whites decreased from 76% in 1970 to 60% in 2014.[40] Unfortunately, the black communities have seen larger changes in these trends and feel the negative effects.

Single-parent households are a significant factor when it comes to crime rates and poverty. As Larry Elder has noted, "Children who grow up without a father are five times more likely to live in poverty and commit crime, nine times more likely to drop out of school, and twenty times more likely to end up in prison."[42]

In a 1995 study, the Heritage Foundation found, "propensity to crime develops in stages associated with major psychological and sociological factors. The factors are not caused by race or poverty, and the stages are the normal tasks of growing up that every child confronts as he gets older. In the case of future violent criminals, these tasks, in the absence of the love, affection, and dedication of both his parents, become perverse exercises, frustrating his needs and stunting his ability to belong."[41]

Other points include:[41]

"Over the past thirty years, the rise in violent crime parallels the rise in families abandoned by fathers."

"High-crime neighborhoods are characterized by high concentrations of families abandoned by fathers."

"State-by-state analysis by Heritage scholars indicates that a 10 percent increase in the percentage of children living in single-parent homes leads typically to a 17 percent increase in juvenile crime."

"The rate of violent teenage crime corresponds with the number of families abandoned by fathers."

It is not wrong for single mothers to get help from extended family or local religious organizations. In fact, these two things can give children good role models and teach children virtue. However, disrupting the nuclear family simply because Black Lives Matter views it as "Western" or "white" is wrong and harmful to the black community. Two-parent households are a positive thing. Women should be encouraged to get married before having children, and men should not be allowed to abandon their responsibilities as a parent.

> "There's no more important ingredient for success. Nothing that would be more important for us (in) reducing violence than strong, stable families, which means we should do more to support marriage and encourage fatherhood."
>
> — Barack Obama[39]

PART 3

WHITE WOKENESS

CHAPTER 1

WHAT MAKES WOKENESS MEANINGLESS

Wokeness- a state of being aware of social problems such as racism and inequality.

A better definition for wokeness is- a way for leftists to virtue signal and feed their own ego.

The year 2020 has got to be the year of the weird woke whites. One of the weirder stories was Chelsea Handler saying she had to remind her ex-boyfriend 50 Cent that he was black. 50 Cent opposed Joe Biden because 50 Cent did not like the idea of having to pay 62% in taxes. Handler's response was told to Jimmy Fallon, "I had to remind him that he was a black person, so he can't vote for Donald Trump." Handler said that she would be willing to "seal the deal in more ways than one" and "go for another spin" with her ex-boyfriend 50 Cent if he denounced President Trump.[96] I don't think 50 Cent needed to be reminded that he was black. I would also like to note that Chelsea Handler is forty-five. Now I'm not saying that 50 Cent can do better. I'm just saying that he can easily get a girl that's half Handler's age, has a better personality, and is not a narcissist.

In 2020, some white people did a weird sort of prayer sessions that acknowledged their white privilege. One of these prayer sessions was done by Mary Ann Williamson (It may have been done while she was running for president). She had white people surround black people and chant some prayer about how white people apologize to blacks for all the evils whites committed. The whole thing was uncomfortable to watch. I don't know how the black people in that audience felt, I just know that it seemed pretty weird to me.

Dan Cathy, the CEO of Chick-fil-A, shined a rapper's shoes. In an interview, Cathy said, "I invite folks to put some words to action, and if we need to find somebody who needs to have their shoes shined, we need to just go right on over and shine their shoes."[95]

Here's the real question. Do you really believe that these acts are designed to help black communities in any way? No. When people posted black squares on social media, did that cure racism? Or did it fix failing public schools? Maybe that lowered the crime rates? No. This was done with one goal in mind, to allow white people to virtue signal and feel good about themselves. And being woke is a great way to virtue signal, feed your ego, and distinguish yourself from others. (By distinguish yourself from others, I mean look like an idiot.)

Woke whites are willing to put on their armor and go to war for the smallest things, as long as they get to flex their moral authority. One example of this occurred in an online meeting of New York City's Community Education Council District 2 on June 29, 2020. Councilor Robin Broshi yelled at fellow councilor Thomas Wrocklage. What was Wrocklage's crime against humanity? During a previous virtual meeting, Wrocklage had a friend's nephew over, and he allowed the nephew to sit in his lap. And the nephew was black.

Unwilling to allow a virtue-signaling opportunity go to waste, Broshi harnessed her inner wokeness and released it on to Wrocklage. "'It hurts people when they see a white man bouncing a brown baby on their lap, and they don't know the context!" Broshi said. "That is harmful! That makes people cry. That makes people log out of our meetings … I'm getting pressure for not being enough of an advocate, and I take that to heart, and that hurts me.'"[25]

For starters, I do not think the context is particularly important. Some people may have thought that the child was his. Others may have thought that he was looking out for someone else's kid. I have confidence that normal people do not look at this and cry. In fact, I will say that this was harmless, and most people did not pay it any mind.

Is Broshi crazy? Yeah, probably. But the heart of the issue is what she says towards the end. Pay attention to the last sentence. She felt that she was not seen as enough of an advocate, and it hurt her. She put real personal value in the social capital gains from being a leftist, and when the social capital is low, that creates a problem. Her solution to this: create a non-issue to show how much of an advocate she is. Nothing was gained from this. Broshi insulted Wrocklage and gained her worthless woke points.

Another example of white virtue signaling is Chris Palmer.[27] Palmer is a former ESPN reporter who cheered on rioters in

Minneapolis. When someone posted a picture of an affordable housing unit on fire, he tweeted, "Burn that shit down. Burn it all down." Unfortunately, a few days later, riots erupted in Los Angeles, and they started getting close to his gated community. He changed his tone pretty quickly and tweeted, "They just attacked our sister community down the street. It's a gated community, and they tried to climb the gates. They had to beat them back. Then destroyed a Starbucks and now are in front of my building. Get these animals TF out of my neighborhood. Go back to where you live …" "Tear up your own shit. Don't come to where we live at and tear our neighborhood up. We care about our community. If you don't care about yours, I don't give a shit," he added.[27]

It is funny how quickly someone's opinion can change. This man is perfectly fine with rioters burning black neighborhoods, as long as he gets to stand on the ashes and call himself an ally. But the second it might impact him at all, he calls it quits. He wants law and order. Suddenly, I bet the cops that he was protesting a few days ago were looking a lot more friendly. It may seem like leftist hypocrisy is at the core of this scenario, but it is Palmer's white guilt that takes center stage.

CHAPTER 2

HEALING WHITE PEOPLE'S FEELINGS

As mentioned in the previous chapter, the American political Left loves to virtue signal about their wokeness and their desire for social justice. Unfortunately, this appeals to American liberals as well as leftists. But why is this so appealing? Why do people like Broshi or Palmer feel the need to virtue signal? What is so virtuous about acknowledging your white privilege?

One of the reasons this is so appealing can be explained through what Shelby Steele calls "white guilt."[49] Steele says white guilt goes back several decades, to the late 1960s when America was beginning to see that racism was immoral. Whites who were forced to see the negative effects of racism were suddenly faced with guilt. They soon realized that they were losing a sense of moral authority. Whites compensated this loss of moral authority by distancing themselves from racism and soon found a virtue in the idea "those whites may have been racist, but I am not. Therefore, I am a good and moral person." White guilt was born. Steele explains,

Because White Guilt is a vacuum of moral authority, it makes the moral authority of whites and the legitimacy of American institutions contingent on proving a negative: that they are not racist. The great power of white guilt comes from the fact that it functions by stigma, like racism itself. Whites and American Institutions are stigmatized as racist until they prove otherwise (*White Guilt,* pg. 27).

White guilt is appealing because nothing needs to change as a result of it. Remember that white guilt is not about righting a wrong or fixing a problem; it is about restoring the moral authority of whites. It is easy to yell "systemic racism" and "white privilege" to show the virtue of disliking racism.

White guilt has changed over time. It has mixed with millennial narcissism and the desire for attention. This has led to young whites making "social justice" a large part of their identity. They make it clear that they are allies to minorities and that no one is going to deny them their identity … not even minorities.

An example of a young white person being an "ally" is a white woman yelling at black police officers and telling them that they are racist. When questioned about it, she responded, "Just because I'm white and I haven't experienced racism myself doesn't mean I can't fight for justice. They're a part of the system. They're a part of the problem. Just because they're black doesn't mean they're not a part of the problem. I'm allowed to say this to whoever. Because I'm white, racism is a white person's problem. Racism is my problem. I need to fix this."[24]

There is a lot one can take away from that encounter. There is the irony of a white woman yelling at blacks and telling blacks that they are racist even though she has never experienced racism. It is also funny that she considers those officers "part of the problem," even though those police officers and many others risk their lives every day to keep that woman (as well as many other people who hate cops) safe. I doubt she would still consider those police officers part of the problem if a criminal were trying to burglarize her home.

I will say that there are bad cops, but the system is good. The system is made of people. They can use reforms to consistently improve the system. For example, allowing police departments more autonomy in the firing of bad cops. But, for a leftist, the entire system is bad, and because the entire system is bad, there can be no good cops. That is why the leftist has no problem saying that the black cops are part of the problem. When you assume that the entire system is wrong, you do not have to account for individuals. You do not have to acknowledge good cops.

Another thing that stands out is the narcissism and sense of self-importance. For starters, she thinks that she can defeat racism, something that has existed across the world for thousands of years. Yeah, I would not hold my breath on that one. The funniest line is, "Racism is my problem. I need to fix this." Wow, isn't she so brave for taking on this burden for humanity? After seeing that act of selflessness, I am surprised she didn't start passing pieces of bread and say, "This bread is of my body. Consume it, and you will be free of racism. For racism is my problem, and it shall be fixed." Narcissism aside, she did not offer any solution. All she did was yell at police officers. Believe it or not, yelling at a problem does not make it go away. If your car gets a flat tire, yelling at the tire is not going to fix it.

The final thing that stands out is the belief that black people have little to no agency. "Racism is my problem. I need to fix this." What, blacks can't speak for themselves? Does she really think that blacks and minorities need her to fix their problems? If she does, this shows racism on the part of the leftist. She believes that whites like her are the only ones capable of 'solving the problem.' It shows a bigotry of low expectations.

There are other examples of whites attacking blacks in order to show that they are allies to the black community.

In July of 2020, a video surfaced of a black man taking down Black Lives Matter posters. He said that he lived across the street and was tired of seeing those posters. While he was taking them down, a white man came and tackled him. The white man then chased the black man out of the area while telling the black man, "Get the fuck out of here, bro" and "This is my park, bro." This woke white man had placed so much stock identifying as a social justice warrior that it became a part of his identity. When someone attacked his ideology, he saw it as an assault on him; therefore, he was willing to attack anyone who opposed his ideas, even if the person he attacks is someone he claims to be fighting for.

How is it possible for a white person to assault a black person for merely disagreeing with leftism and the white person believes that they still hold the moral high ground? Steele explains this through what he calls "white blindness." "White blindness is an unconscious self-absorption by which whites see racial issues ... as opportunities to dissociate from historic racism. Thus, encountering the black face is more an opportunity to dissociate than to see the human being like oneself." (*White Guilt*, pg. 129).

When these whites attacked blacks, they did not see the hypocrisy in these attacks because they cared more about their image than anything else. The white blindness allowed them to maintain the idea that they were justified in these actions because they believed it disassociated them from racism.

Unfortunately, many whites think this way. It is even more unfortunate when woke whites try to act on behalf of blacks and demand things that black Americans do not want.

In July of 2020, a Gallup poll stated that most blacks wanted to maintain the number of police in their neighborhoods; some wanted to increase the police presence. Sixty-one percent of black Americans said they wanted police to spend the same amount of time in their neighborhoods. Another 20% wanted law enforcement to spend more time in their streets.[51] That is 81% of black Americans surveyed want the same police presence or more police in their neighborhoods. Of the blacks who claimed they saw police often in their neighborhoods, 66% said they wanted the same or more police presence (56% wanted the same, 10% wanted more). Of the blacks who claimed they saw police sometimes, 84% said they wanted the same presence level or more (60% same amount of time, 24% more time).

Some Black Lives Matter activists have entertained the idea of abolishing the police altogether. Gallup polls noted that only 22 percent of black Americans support calls to abolish police departments.[50] There is an obvious disconnect between these woke activists and the general public. It is unfortunate that some of these people find their way into power.

CHAPTER 3

WOKE POLITICIANS

It is not hard for me to believe that many politicians are not good at their jobs. I don't think America puts forth her best and brightest to lead (with a few exceptions). So, it is not a surprise that there are the typical liars, hypocrites, and just plain stupid politicians (you will see plenty of the last one in this chapter.) Somehow, woke politicians have found ways to make politicians even more unlikable.

Why are woke politicians worse than an average politician? Because despite everything, a well-meaning politician can have an admirable goal, "to seek the overall wellbeing of their constituents." This is typically done by making the city safer or trying to bring prosperity to local communities. These means are secondary to woke politicians. What they want is to virtue signal and push identity politics.

A good example of this is what progressive politicians did to a project in New York City in 2020. It is no secret that New York was hit hard by the pandemic. Many people lost their lives due to coronavirus. Eventually, the economy in New York City fell to pieces. When unemployment was at 16% in NYC, this project seemed to be something that everyone could see that the city needed. After all, it would add an estimated 20,000 jobs to the NYC economy. It would also help develop an underdeveloped industrial section. Woke politicians adamantly opposed the project. What was their reason? Emma Fitzsimmons with the *New York Times* wrote,[94] "the area's councilman and some community groups opposed the rezoning, saying that it would be a "luxury mall" that would worsen gentrification, and contending that job estimates were inflated."[94] In English, the woke politicians opposed a project that could have helped many people because they did not want to risk white people going into the area. Are you starting to see why woke politicians are bad?

When the average person goes woke, there is not much of an impact. There is the usual grandstanding and virtue signaling on social media. Unfortunately, wokeness has found its way into the political system. It is dangerous when politicians go woke because they can oversee the governing of thousands, perhaps millions of people. When politicians are more interested in virtue signaling than doing their jobs, the citizens will be the ones who pay the price.

Bill de Blasio

It should not be a surprise that NYC mayor Bill de Blasio is on this list. I noted back in Part 2 that in June 2020, NYC saw a large increase in its crime rates. Bill de Blasio also cut a billion dollars from the NYPD and disbanded an anti-crime unit. Unsurprisingly, July 2020 also saw large increases in the murder and shootings compared to the previous year. The murder rate rose 58.8% (34 in July 2019, 54 in July 2020), and shooting incidents rose 177.3% (88 July 2019, 244 July 2020).[52] There were 39 murders in June of 2020, compared to the 54 murders in July of 2020. That is a 38.4% increase in one month. June 2020 had 205 shooting incidents; July 2020 had 244 for a 19% increase in one month.

But this crime increase is not the only reason why de Blasio is on this list. In July, de Blasio painted "Black Lives Matter" on the street outside of Trump Tower. De Blasio even allowed the mural to skip the permit process. He was eager to show his support for the movement and grandstand. Bill de Blasio himself went and helped paint "Black Lives Matter" outside Brooklyn Borough Hall. He used city resources to maintain the murals. When people vandalized the murals, he sent DOT officials to repaint them. On July 13, 2020, de Blasio tweeted, "To whoever vandalized our mural on 5th Avenue: nice try. @NYC_DOT has already fixed it. The #BlackLivesMatter movement is more than words, and it can't be undone."

Bill de Blasio could have attempted to stop the crime wave. He could have changed his anti-cop perspective and hired more police. Instead, he chose to virtue signal, and this proved costly.

On July 12, there was a shooting at a barbeque, which left three people injured and one dead. The person who died was one-year-old Davell Gardner. When asked about this de Blasio said the following, "It's not something we can ever look away from," he said. "It's something we have to address and stop."

What makes me angry is that de Blasio looked away. He did not address or stop the violence. He showed more interest in protecting a mural that says "Black Lives Matter" than protecting black lives in his city. And that is one of the problems that is at the heart of leftist politicians. These politicians do not have to deal with the consequences of their actions. That is why it is so easy for the politicians to virtue signal rather than govern effectively. It would not matter if half of NYC is unemployed and living in poverty, de Blasio would get paid his $258,750 salary. It does not matter that violent crime is rising in NYC. Bill de Blasio will always have safety and security for him and his family.

Bill de Blasio says that the Black Lives Matter movement is more than words. Politicians like him are nothing but words. And those words, much like the politicians, are utterly useless.

Minneapolis City Council

As you know, Minneapolis is the city where George Floyd was killed. It was ground zero for the riots. Nearly 1500 businesses in the Twin Cities region were burned, looted, or vandalized. The damage is believed to exceed $500 million.[67] The Minneapolis government could have taken a firm stance against the violence. Instead, government officials tried to virtue signal. It did not work for mayor Jacob Frey. He attended a BLM rally and tried to "admit his shortcomings" (although, he was probably talking about his shortcomings with white privilege and not his short comings as mayor). However, one of the speakers demanded an answer on whether Frey supported the abolishment of the police. When he said he did not support the full abolishment of the police department, the crowd booed and drove Frey out of the rally.

The Minneapolis City Council was more agreeable. In June of 2020, the Minneapolis City Council voted 12-0 to abolish the city's police department.[68] It did not automatically lead to the abolishment of the Minneapolis PD, but it was the first step needed to get rid of the police.

This did raise concerns over who would keep the citizens of Minneapolis safe. City Council President Lisa Bender was quick to run to the defense of the proposal. In a CNN interview, Bender was asked, "Do you understand that the word, dismantle, or police-free also makes some people nervous, for instance? What if, in the middle of the night, my home is broken into? Who do I call?" Bender responded, "Yes, I mean, I hear that loud and clear from a lot of my neighbors. And I know—and myself, too, and I know that that comes from a place of privilege. Because for those of us for whom the system is working, I think we need to step back and imagine what it would feel like to already live in that reality where calling the police may mean more harm is done."[69]

Wow, that is some grade-A thinking there. Next time your house is being broken into, acknowledge your privilege. Maybe then you and the burglar can become best friends over it. Yeah ... no. That doesn't work in the real world. In the real world, you get injured or killed, and you get your car or tv stolen. Call me old-fashioned, but if someone is threatening my safety or my family's safety, I don't care what happens to them.

But maybe I'm wrong. Maybe I don't know how to live without the privilege of the police. Surely, members of the Minneapolis City Council are willing to be without police, especially since they voted to abolish them. Well no. It turns out some of the councilors were not feeling safe from the rise in crime. As a result, the city of Minneapolis provided private security for council members Phillipe Cunningham, Alondra Cano, and Andrea Jenkins.[70] Taxpayers were paying $4,500 a day to keep these members safe. Apparently, you need to work for the government to be important enough to protect. And the worst part is that I don't think these councilors acknowledged their privilege.

What happens when your city is run by incompetent, hypocritical elitists who take the side of rioters? Crime goes up while your city goes down the toilet. As of September 15, 2020, Minneapolis has seen a large increase in crime compared to the year before. Homicide increased by 87% (rising from 30 in 2019 to 56 in 2020). Robbery increased by 37% (rising from 931 in 2019 to 1275 in 2020). Aggravated assault rose 20% (1,750 in 2019 to 2,100 in 2020).[71]

In August of 2020, the Minneapolis PD offered tips to citizens for their safety. The tips included:[72]

- Do not walk alone
- Be hyper-aware of your surroundings at all times—pay attention!
- Carry only items you need, and carry less cash
- Be prepared to give up your cell phone and purse/wallet
- Have keys already in your hand as you approach your car
- Despite all our efforts, robberies may still occur! Do not argue or fight with the criminal. Do as they say. Your safety is most important!

It would be wise for the people of Minneapolis to vote these councilors out of office as soon as they get the chance. Sure, the councilors showed that they were allies to the BLM Movement. All it took was councilors taking the side of violent rioters, voting to abolish the police and cause a Ferguson effect in Minneapolis. And most importantly, they put the people of Minneapolis in danger.

Jenny Durkan

Like many major cities, Seattle saw protests following George Floyd's death. The protests turned violent. Police noted that rocks, bottles, and "explosives" were thrown at them. They used non-violent methods such as tear gas, pepper spray, and flashbangs to push back against the violence. Unfortunately, the city tended to be more concerned with the comfort of the rioters. The city sided with the rioters on several occasions; one example is when the city banned the police from using tear gas to disperse large, violent crowds.

On June 8, 2020, Seattle Police abandoned the East Precinct. Rioters took over the area and named it the Capital Hill Autonomous Zone or CHAZ (the name was later changed to the Capital Hill Organized Protests or CHOP).

A few days later, Seattle Mayor Jenny Durkan went on CNN to address the CHOP. When asked how long this could last, Durkan said that Seattle could be in for "a summer of love." Durkan also said, "The police will be policing in there. I want to be very clear on that. Our chief of police was in there assessing today. We take public safety very seriously. We met with businesses and residents today. We don't have to sacrifice public safety for First Amendment rights. Both can exist, and we'll make sure that both exist in Seattle."[43]

This was proven false over the next couple of weeks. CHOP saw a large increase in vandalism and violence. Seattle Police Chief Carmen Best noted that 911 police response times had tripled in the area since the CHOP was established.[45] Local businesses sued the city for the handling of the CHOP. The businesses said in the civil suit,

The City has acknowledged the serious safety issues it has created, in particular noting that there are 'dangerous conditions' at night, but the City has nonetheless chosen to maintain its policy of providing resources and support to the CHOP occupiers. The City's conduct has enabled the widespread destruction and vandalism of private property. Graffiti is pervasive throughout CHOP—it is not only on barriers, streets, sidewalks, but also on nearly every private building within CHOP. Graffiti that is painted over almost immediately returns, and property owners have been told by CHOP participants that if they dare to paint over graffiti, their buildings will be more severely vandalized or even burned to the ground … Plaintiffs and others have repeatedly pleaded with Mayor Durkan and others to cease enabling the destruction of their property, and the imminent danger posed to them and their neighborhood. But the city has not listened or has not cared, and plaintiffs have had to resort to litigation to make themselves heard.[44]

The vandalism and destruction of property is not the worst part of the CHOP. In the weeks of CHOP, there were multiple shootings.[46] On June 20, Lorenzo Anderson, 19, was shot and killed in the area. About a week later, a 16-year-old male and a 14-year-old male were shot. The 16-year-old died of his injuries, and the 14-year-old was in critical condition. The 14-year old's condition improved to serious.

The CHOP was cleared on July 1, 2020, when Durkan gave an executive order to clear the area. It can be argued that Durkan saw the violence of the CHOP and realized the public safety hazard. I argue that she cleared CHOP because the protests hit her close to home. Literally. The night before Durkan issued her executive order, members of CHOP gathered outside of Durkan's house. Regardless of Durkan's reasons, she should have acted weeks before. She could have done her duty as mayor and protected her citizens. Instead, she chose to attempt to reason with unreasonable people. And her inaction and desire for virtue signaling cost her city thousands in damages and multiple lives.

All these politicians have several things in common. For starters, they are incompetent. That much is obvious to anyone who pays attention to the damage they allowed to the cities they looked after. But there is something else they have in common. They have a desire to virtue signal. Usually, it is about how open, accepting they are and not at all racist. And the citizens of their cities pay the price. As I conclude this chapter, I would like to note a few other problems I have with these virtue-signaling politicians.

First, something that does not make sense is that many of these politicians make claims of widespread or systemic racism. Yet, the same politicians usually want to increase the power the government has, thereby increasing the power of the system. I find it strange that the same people who say how evil America was in the past want to give more power to the government today. If there is a tyrannical, racist, and oppressive government, why is the answer to give more power to the government? If leftist politicians are so concerned about systemic racism, why not give up their own power to a minority? If these politicians are so upset about systemic racism, then they should step down from their elected positions of power. But that is unlikely to happen.

It seems to me that these politicians are after two things—ensuring that they get elected or reelected, and maximizing their personal power.

Second, when politicians say that there is systemic racism in the United States, they end up calling themselves racist. These politicians make the system. They are the ones that have the power to make the laws and the rules for society. That's all. I just find it funny when someone tries to virtue signal, and they end up making themselves look bad.

Third, politicians are wrong when they suggest that there are systems that should be torn down. In 2020, a lot of this was directed towards the police. The criminal justice system may be flawed, but it is not broken. There is a difference between saying that a system is flawed and a system is broken. If the system is flawed, then it can be improved by fixing the flaws. There are flaws in the criminal justice system. But the system can be gradually improved. A couple of things that can help is giving police more control over the hiring and firing of bad cops. But some politicians suggest that the system is broken. If the entire system is corrupted, then it can't be fixed. At that point, the only thing to do is tear the system down. What happens when foolish politicians try to tear down a system that is essential and not broken? We saw what happens when people pushed to defund or abolish the police.

Finally, politicians make claims of institutional or systemic racism, but they have the power to make changes to the system. If you can find a law that is clearly racist, then why not change it? It would not be hard to examine these laws and make the case to the American people on why it should be changed. The problem for these politicians is that there are no laws that allow for racial discrimination. Since these politicians cannot find a specific law, they resort to broad and vague terms (such as systemic racism). If you ask one of these leftist politicians, "What is racist about the system today?" The answer will be along the lines of "everything … racism is completely embedded in our country." This line of thinking is what brings us to the next chapter.

CHAPTER 4

WHITE FRAGILITY

White Fragility is a *New York Times* best-selling book written by Robin DiAngelo. I found it necessary to devote an entire chapter to this book because it is a topic for significant discussion in the United States. I find the logic in this book flawed and three steps in the wrong direction. How would I describe DiAngelo? I would say she is a mix of Barb Kellner (from the Introduction) and the crazy cat lady from *The Simpsons.*

Before I explain white fragility, let me give some context about DiAngelo. Many of the personal experiences she talks about come from when she was a diversity trainer. DiAngelo would go into a firm and give lectures. These lectures would say that all white people are racist. White people would get offended and respond negatively to DiAngelo's claim. The negative responses ranged from anger, sadness, defensiveness, withdrawal, etc. These negative responses form what DiAngelo calls "white fragility." This white fragility is a way for whites to "maintain our dominance within the racial hierarchy (pg. 2)."

Let me summarize that for you. Robin DiAngelo goes into a firm and calls white people racist. White people are uncomfortable and offended at the accusation of racism because racism is perceived as a major insult. DiAngelo's response is essentially, "These white people sure do get offended when I call them racist. This is because whites are fragile on the topic of race." The concept of white fragility is nothing more than an attempt to dismiss anyone who disagrees with DiAngelo.

DiAngelo notes that she was confused in the early days of her lectures. After all, who would not want to get told they are racist? She then realized something. "And in light of so many white expressions of resentment toward people of color, I realized that we see ourselves as entitled to, and deserving of, more than people of color deserve ..." (pg. 3). First, the resentment DiAngelo experienced is not toward people of color. It is toward her. The people were resentful of DiAngelo, and she just used people of color as a shield. Also, I do not know where she gets the idea that white people believe they are more entitled and deserving than blacks. I do not think it is a widespread opinion that whites deserve more than blacks based on skin color alone. She mentions that there is an investment to protect the system that benefits whites. The problem with that argument is that system we live under is designed to allow anyone who makes good choices to prosper. Skin color is not an important factor in the system. The important factors are things like hours worked, education, whether the person is married or not.[55]

You may think that DiAngelo is simply misunderstood and that she is the best person to lead the conversation. Wrong. DiAngelo practically admits she is not qualified to discuss these issues. "For example, I can be seen as qualified to lead a major or minor organization in this country with no understanding whatsoever of perspectives or experiences of people of color, few if any relationships with people of color, and virtually no ability to engage critically with the topic of race"(pg. 8). I do not know why she admitted this. She could have left this part out, and the paragraph would have been unchanged. If I had to guess, she did it for one of two reasons.

1. To show some form of white privilege or
2. To treat ignorance and stupidity like she treats racism

The fact that DiAngelo speaks to these organizations does show me that something is wrong, but it is not white privilege. It is the stupidity of the organizations. Organizations do not need people like DiAngelo to go and berate white people for an hour. These organizations have the power to hire whomever they want and can dictate codes of conduct in workplaces. Organizations should not hire people for the sole purpose of "increasing diversity". That's just a type of tokenism. Organizations should focus on bringing in employees who bring something to the table. A great example is a woman I used to work with named Tekeisha. She was hardworking, kind, caring, compassionate, great at her job, and just a pleasure to be around. Patients and fellow employees loved her. I do not think there was a day that she was not smiling or making me smile. When I was sad about something, she cheered me up. When I was happy, she found a way to make me happier. People like Tekeisha are what organizations should focus on. Skin color is not important. What is important is seeing what the employee brings to the table, both for the company and the people the company serves.

Treating ignorance and stupidity like she treats racism is another possible reason. DiAngelo faces racism with the idea that if you admit you are a racist, that makes you better somehow. Admitting you do not know what you are talking about does not mean you know more about a topic. It certainly does not give you any level of expertise. And it does not give you any moral high ground. It means you probably should not speak on the issue. Say you have a sick child. Would you take your child to a pediatrician who cannot stand being around children, has virtually no experience, and lacks the ability to think critically when it comes to diagnosing and treating illnesses? I know I would not. I would think that most people would not trust someone like that either. Then again, *White Fragility* was a best-selling book, so maybe stupidity sells.

One of the many examples of stupidity is DiAngelo's definition of a white progressive. "I believe that white progressives cause the most daily damage to people of color. I define white progressive as white people who think they are not racist, or are less racist, or in the 'choir,' or already 'gets it'" (pg. 5). This is a fancy way of saying all white people are racist. Aside from old-school open racists and members of the Alt-right, white people do not consider themselves racist. Therefore, this definition includes most white people because most white people think they are not racist (and they are probably right).

What's more, by this definition, Robin DiAngelo considers me a white progressive. It is funny that she considers me a progressive because I am a pro-life, gun-loving, big government-hating Republican. If you are a white person reading this book, chances are she sees you as a white progressive. I guess every white person from Donald Trump to Bernie Sanders is a white progressive in her eyes. There is a reason why DiAngelo is so broad with her terminology. It is in the first sentence, "I believe that white progressives cause the most daily damage to people of color ..." When you say that white progressives cause the most damage and classify nearly everyone as a white progressive, that is one way she comes to the idea of systemic racism. Not by finding actual racist practices, but by shifting the goalposts to match her beliefs.

One of the biggest issues I have with DiAngelo is that she generalizes. "As a sociologist, I am quite comfortable in generalizing" (pg. 12). I do not generalize; I try to use data and statistics to show trends in groups of people, but I do not suggest that some or most people's actions indicate that everyone in that group thinks the same. For the most part, generalization is both foolish and lazy. If you have not noticed yet, I hate generalization, especially when it comes to matters of race. Why? Because generalization is at the basis of white supremacy. A white supremacist will look at crime rates or unemployment in the black community. They will see that the rates are different than those for whites. Then they assume that all blacks are violent or lazy. And finally, you end up with white supremacists claiming their membership in the "dominant race." As I said, generalization is foolish, lazy, and even dangerous. Yet, DiAngelo has no problem generalizing if she gets to generalize the right kind of person.

Shockingly (sarcasm), the generalizing DiAngelo does not believe in individualism. She sees it as a way for racists to keep the racial hierarchies in order. "The racial ideology that circulates in the United States rationalizes racial hierarchies as the outcome of a natural order resulting from either genetics or individual effort or talent. Those who do not succeed are just not naturally capable, deserving, or hardworking." The problem with DiAngelo's argument is that she combines the idea of natural talent with hard work, but the two are not the same. I once heard someone say, "If you are not good at something, put a thousand hours of practice into it, and you will at least get kind of good at it." We can't control our natural abilities or what people think we deserve. What we can control is how much effort we put into something. Hard work is crucial to be good at something. The best example I can give is the greatest basketball player of all time, Michael Jordan. Jordan did not come into the world as the best basketball player of all time. He did not spring from the womb and then proceed to dunk a basketball from the free-throw line. Hell, he did not even make his high school sophomore varsity basketball team. How did he become great? He practiced ... hard. The summer he did not make the basketball team, he practiced all summer. When he was at North Carolina, he worked hard to continue his improvement. When the Bulls front office saw how hard Jordan practiced, they knew they made a good choice in drafting him. Every coach who coached Michael Jordan praised his work ethic. Michael Jordan was not great due to natural talent; he was great because he was always willing to work hard to improve himself. Hard work is not a tool for racial hierarchy. It is something that is necessary to improve yourself as time goes forward. And that effort is the only thing that you can control.

DiAngelo believes that racism affects everything, even our institutions. But what happens when people of color begin to hold power in these institutions? (In the book, she mentions Barack Obama, Marco Rubio, Clarence Thomas, Colin Powell.)

According to DiAngelo, "they support the status quo and do not challenge racism in any way significant enough to be threatening" (pg27). First off, what is the status quo these people are maintaining? Like everyone else in the US, these people were chosen to do a job. For example, Marco Rubio's duty is to the people of Florida. It is his job to represent his constituents to the best of his ability. Also, what does it look like when racism is challenged? What would Obama had to have done to threaten racism (at least by DiAngelo's standards)? My guess. If Obama hired DiAngelo for a couple of diversity events, he would have been the one who broke the status quo. It does not matter for DiAngelo. The institutions are run by whites, and I guess are a tool of white supremacy.

She lists the following for 2016-2017 (pg. 31) :

- Ten richest Americans: 100 percent white (seven of whom are among the ten richest in the world)
- US Congress: 90 percent white
- US governors: 96 percent white
- Top military advisors: 100 percent white
- President and vice president: 100 percent white
- US House Freedom Caucus: 99 percent white
- Current US Cabinet: 91 percent white
- People who decide which tv shows we see: 93 percent white
- People who decide which books we read: 90 percent white
- People who decide which news is covered: 8 5 percent white
- People who decide which music is produced: 95 percent white

- People who directed the one hundred top-grossing films of all time, worldwide: 95 percent white
- Teachers: 82 percent white
- Full-time college professors: 84 percent white
- Owners of men's professional football teams: 97 percent white

In true fashion, DiAngelo goes full Barb Kellner on this list. For many of these things, there can be factors other than race that play a role. I also question the impact of some of the institutions on this list.

"Ten richest Americans: 100 percent white"- This does not have anything to do with race. People become wealthy by providing valuable goods and services to others. For example, Jeff Bezos is the founder and CEO of Amazon. The fact that he is white is irrelevant. He made it possible for nearly any tangible good to be a click away.

"US Congress: 90 percent white"- In 2019, Whites made up 78% of Congress. According to the Pew Research Center, the percentage of whites in Congress has declined over the last couple of decades.[58]

"US governors: 96 percent white"- Factors that play a part in the election of governors include tax plans, government programs, goals while in office, candidate communication skills, etc.

"Top military advisors: 100 percent white" as well as "Current US Cabinet: 91 percent white"- This has nothing to do with race. The advisors are chosen for knowledge and experience.

"President and vice president: 100 percent white"- In 2012, this was 50%. In 2021, it will be 50%.

"US House Freedom Caucus: 99 percent white"- The Congressional Black Caucus has 0 percent whites.

"People who decide which TV shows we see: 93 percent white"- In my opinion, TV does not have the impact that it used to have. Young people today are more influenced by social media, video games, and other entertainment platforms.

"People who decide which books we read: 90 percent white"- I'm not sure what she means by this. I assume she means that whites run 90 percent of major publishers. In any case, it did not stop DiAngelo's book from being published or *How to Be an Antiracist* by Ibram X. Kendi. If the book has the ability to sell, it will be published.

"People who decide which news is covered: 85 percent white"- Trust in the mainstream news media has declined over the last couple of years. People have noticed a bias and have looked to other sources for news. There is a rise in alternative news media, for example, Tim Pool at timcast.com

"People who decide which music is produced: 95 percent white"- "WAP" by Cardi B ... enough said.

"People who directed the one hundred top-grossing films of all time, worldwide: 95 percent white"- This is just saying that some of the most successful movies were directed by white people. Also, you run the risk of seeing the same director multiple times. For example- At least two of Christopher Nolan's movies are on this list.[59]

"Teachers: 82 percent white" and "Full-time college professors: 84 percent white"- This can be explained by supply and demand in the labor markets.

"Owners of men's professional football teams: 97 percent white" — A professional football team is difficult to buy.

Owners may not be willing to sell their team. Even if an owner was willing to sell the team, these teams are worth billions of dollars. The last team that was bought in the NFL was the Carolina Panthers (sold for 2.2 billion dollars).

"What about schools? What made a school good?" (pg. 35). DiAngelo does not answer the question. She just asks a bunch of questions directed toward white people (wealthy whites) that try to make the school they went to seem racist. Fortunately, it is not hard to say what makes a school good; no, the number of white people is not a factor. A school's quality can be measured by graduation rates, state test scores, mathematical ability, school safety, school programs, and quality of teachers. DiAngelo also goes on to talk about how our schools are racially segregated. And what's worse, she does not mention the harm to blacks who go to failing schools. She offers no solutions; she just talks about how whites negatively view black schools. Here is my rebuttal. First, public schools are not segregated based on race. They are separated based on the tax areas. That being said, this system fails low-income families who have bad schools. A lot of these parents are forced to send their kids to these failing schools. Parents have been arrested for trying to send their kids to public schools outside of their district. Like I mentioned in previous parts, education is very important. So, this system is setting these kids up to fail.

Unlike DiAngelo, I will offer a couple of solutions. One solution is the opening of charter schools. These schools can be an alternative to failing public schools. Charter schools can allow for teachers to be innovative in their approach to education. Since most charter schools do not work with the teacher's union, they have more flexibility. The most important aspect of the charter school is that it offers competition and gives parents a choice. Eva Moskowitz, CEO of Success Academy Charter schools, said, "What we prove is that there is nothing wrong with the children, there is something wrong with the system. A monopolistic system that is not allowing kids to succeed."[61] Another solution is school choice and school vouchers. School choice will allow parents to send their kids to any public school, regardless of district. This helps parents that do not want to send their kids to failing schools. School vouchers will change the way schools are funded. Instead of schools being funded by property taxes in a district, schools will be funded by the number of students in its school. In theory, if parents can send their kids (and school funding) to any school, good schools will see more students and receive more resources. Failing schools will see fewer students and funding and have to change to compete. This can help families by giving them access to better education opportunities.

DiAngelo then makes claims of white supremacy in healthcare. "When my parents read their birthing manuals and other written materials, the pictures most likely depicted primarily white mothers and fathers, doctors and nurses ... The years of research demonstrating racial discrimination in health care assure me that my parents were more likely to have been treated well by hospital personnel and to receive a higher caliber of care than would people of color" (pg. 52). The pictures of white people in the birthing manuals are not white supremacy. It's just trying to appeal to as many people as possible. Since whites made up a majority of the population, the birthing manuals probably put whites there to appeal to the majority of the population. As a former health care worker,

I take offense to the idea that people of color receive a lower caliber of health care due to race. DiAngelo does not offer any quantifiable information to back up this claim. In fact, she co-authored the source she cites for this claim. ("Addressing Whiteness in Nursing Education The Sociopolitical Climate Project at the University of Washington School of Nursing" by Carole Schroeder and Robin DiAngelo). The paper she cites does not have anything to do with the quality of health care patients receive. The paper is about the "whiteness in academic nursing".[62] The paper (much like white fragility) is pure garbage. The solution to the "whiteness in academic nursing" is more diversity workshops. My boiling point for this was when DiAngelo said, "Based on this hierarchy, we could predict whether I would survive my birth based on my race" (pg. 52). I don't know what she is claiming on this one. Maybe she is implying that doctors do not care about black babies. Whatever she assumes (like everything else), she is wrong. I can speak firsthand that whites are not guaranteed survival. I had a nephew who did not survive his birth (yes, he was white). I barely survived my birth. I was born roughly two months premature; the doctors told my father that if I survived the first night, I would have a better chance of survival. But it was touch and go. If not for modern technology, I would probably be dead. It is worth noting that the infant mortality rate is higher for blacks (10.8 deaths per 1000) than it is for whites (4.9 deaths per 1000); the group with the lowest infant mortality rate is Asian Americans at (3.6 deaths per 1000). But the issue is not racism. According to the CDC, "Over 21,000 infants died in the United States in 2018. The five leading causes of infant death in 2018 were:

1. Birth defects.
2. Preterm birth and low birth weight.
3. Maternal pregnancy complications.
4. Sudden infant death syndrome.
5. Injuries.[63]

So far, DiAngelo has said that white supremacy exists in all our institutions, schools, and in the healthcare industry. What else could DiAngelo consider racist? How about owning a gun to defend your home? On pages 44 and 45, DiAngelo talks about a couple she knew of who moved to New Orleans. They bought a house for $25,000. Shockingly, the neighborhood was not very safe. The wife did not feel safe to go outside, and the couple bought a gun to defend their home. DiAngelo does not like that the couple bought a gun because the couple moved into a black neighborhood. There are two problems I have with DiAngelo's story and why these people are "racist." 1. Her explanation of why the house is cheap. 2. She dismissed the need for a gun.

DiAngelo explains why the house is cheap. "Notice the need for a gun is a key part of this story. It would not have the degree of social capital it holds if the emphasis were on the price of the house alone. Rather, the story's emotional power rests on why a house would be that cheap—because it is in a black neighborhood where white people literally might not get out alive" (pg. 44).

So, the house is cheap because white people do not like it? No. Allow me to give you a quick lesson in basic economics. (God knows DiAngelo needs one.) One factor that determines the market price for a good or service is the demand for the product. Factors that influence demand for a house include housing infrastructure, area development, crime rates, emergency response times, etc.

When these factors are negative (high-crime, underdeveloped area, etc.), this leads to a decrease in demand (fewer people find the product desirable). As a result of demand being decreased, the price of the product will decrease (assuming all else remains constant). To summarize, if you decrease the demand for a product, you will see a decrease in the price. It is not racism; it is the market trying to adapt to lower demand. For example, think of Ramen noodles. They taste okay, but they are unhealthy and can probably get old fast if you eat them every day. What makes them so desirable? A pack of five costs about $1.50. Would you buy a pack of Ramen noodles for over $5? Probably not. It is the same concept for the house. People did not buy the house for $100,000 because it was not worth it to them. The sellers did not try to sell the product for $100,000 because they knew that no one would buy it at that price.

Now on to the issue of the gun. "Readers may be asking themselves, 'But if the neighborhood is really dangerous, why is acknowledging this danger a sign of racism?' Research in implicit bias has shown that perceptions of criminal activity are influenced by race. White people will perceive danger simply by the presence of black people; we cannot trust our perceptions when it comes to race and crime" (pg. 45). DiAngelo is saying that this couple wanting to have the ability to defend themselves is racist. It does not matter that there may be high crime rates (the house is in New Orleans, so it probably does), because white people apparently can't sense danger. For starters, there is nothing wrong with wanting to protect yourself, your family, or your property. Wanting to have the tools needed to defend yourself in case of danger is just rational thinking. I was taught that if someone is breaking into your home or is trying to harm you, reach for the gun, not the phone, because you do not know if the cops will get to you before the criminal does. Even if the couple did not need the gun, there is an old saying, "It is better to have a gun and not need it than need it and not have it." This explanation for why this couple should not own a gun is nothing more than DiAngelo preaching to us from her ivory tower. She may not know this, but not everyone lives in a gated community and has high levels of safety. Some people live in unsafe areas. Others live in areas that have slow emergency response times. Some people live in both. And for these people, a gun can be the difference between life and death because a violent criminal will not politely wait for the police to show up.

As I close out this chapter, I will note that DiAngelo is a racist. It is something that she admits. "I know that because I was socialized as white in a racism-based society, I have a racist worldview, deep racial bias, racist patterns and investments in the racist system that has elevated me. Still, I don't feel guilty about racism. I didn't choose this socialization, and it could not be avoided" (pg. 149). A stunning confession. But the truth is that I did not need this quote to know that DiAngelo is a racist. Whether it is the story about DiAngelo worrying about attending a party with black people or her low expectations for blacks, her racism is obvious. Her expectations for blacks are low because she sees blacks as incapable. DiAngelo (like many woke whites) does not respect black people. She pities them. She sees blacks as helpless little sheep that need her help. All while she uses blacks as tokens to call all white people racist. All while flaunting her moral superiority over the rest of us. That raises the question. "Why should I listen to Robin DiAngelo on matters of race?" You shouldn't. Taking advice on racism from DiAngelo is like taking dating advice from a registered sex offender.

What is the purpose of the book *White Fragility*? It is designed to deflect blame and personal responsibility away from DiAngelo's racism. She admits to her racism, but she blames society. She thinks she has made a massive discovery about white people, but all she is doing is projecting her personal views of racism on everyone else. She has the idea that because she is a racist, then everyone is a racist. But, because she is a racist who admits her part in the racist system (that does not exist), she is better than everyone else. She may be part of the problem, but she is the solution to the problem. She can be a model for white people. That is not an exaggeration. She says, "... I would appreciate receiving the feedback publicly, as it is important for white people to see that I am also engaged in a lifelong process of learning and growth. And I could model for other white people how to receive feedback openly and without defensiveness" (pg. 140).

DiAngelo is just like the "racism is my problem. I need to fix this" woman from a couple of chapters ago. I would say DiAngelo is just as foolish and self-absorbed. The concept of White Fragility is the result of DiAngelo not connecting with her audience. When she talked to people as a diversity trainer, people did not respond positively to being called racist. But she still had to justify her job. To do this, she attempted to back people into a corner. The line of thought goes like this.

You need to pay thousands of dollars so that you can listen to DiAngelo tell you that you are a racist. If you listen, then it shows that you acknowledge the racism that is within you. You may be a racist bigot, but at least you know that you are a racist bigot. If you don't listen or get upset at DiAngelo calling you racist, you are fragile about your own racism. The reason you express negative emotions is so you can rationalize your dominance in the racial hierarchy. Therefore, when you get upset at DiAngelo for calling you a racist, you are contributing to the racist system. You are a racist bigot. This is just DiAngelo attempting to create a no-win situation.

Fortunately, DiAngelo is not able to effectively prove her point of systemic racism. She does not take any other potential factors into consideration. DiAngelo automatically assumes that if there is any sort of disparity, there is racism and oppression right around the corner. She uses little to no quantifiable information in her book to support her outlandish claims. What little she does use can be explained with logic and reason, two things that DiAngelo lacks.

PART 4

SOLUTIONS

CONSERVATIVES

Many issues worry conservatives. The rise of socialism, the denial of God, the weakening of American institutions, and political correctness are things that I worry about. But what scares me more than anything is how the Left is targeting the American youth. For this chapter, the main thesis is simple—watch out for your kids. I will note three things that conservative parents should watch out for: indoctrination, misinformation, and a potential rise of pedophilia.

Indoctrination

I am quick to criticize the failures of public education. I briefly discussed this in Part 3. The failures of the education system are real. One example is a recent survey that showed that young Americans do not know the extent of the Holocaust.[73] Roughly two-thirds of the people surveyed did not know that six million Jews were killed during the Holocaust. Furthermore, of the people surveyed, more than one in ten believed the Jews caused the Holocaust.

But this is about more than the inefficiencies and failures of the public education system. There are people in the education system trying to indoctrinate American youth into its ways of thinking. These activists, who call themselves "teachers," are pushing ideologies like White Fragility and Black Lives Matter in schools.

I wrote Part 2 to discuss the concepts and problems that the Black Lives Matter movement causes, and I am not just talking about the riots. Now, Black Lives Matter is trying to get into schools. The following is what BLM demands,[74] "... educators in the BLM at School movement developed these demands for the movement:

1. End "zero tolerance" discipline and implement restorative justice
2. Hire more black teachers
3. Mandate black history and ethnic studies in K-12 curriculum
4. Fund counselors, not cops"

What is most alarming is the K-12 curriculum. The same people who want to dismantle the nuclear family and claim that the United States is systemically racist want to be involved in teaching your children. People like this want to take advantage of children's trusting nature. They want to teach their ideas of intersectional victimhood hierarchies. They want to tell black children that they are victims of the white supremacist system. They want to tell white children that they are guilty of benefiting from a system built on white supremacy. What do you think you get from this? A generation that is more open-minded and understanding? No. You will end up with a generation that is foolish, angry, bitter, and resentful. Keep in mind, the people burning the American cities in 2020 did so under the banner of Black Lives Matter.

Even if BLM does not get into schools, there are still plenty of teachers willing to teach it anyway. In an old campus reform video, a teacher said the following, "... I'm teaching children social studies that's not in our curricula. I'm teaching them things about how to be an anti-racist. Instead of teaching those same three famous black people that we continue to teach, I taught them about protesting. I taught them about Black Lives Matter."[75]

This indoctrination was somewhat hampered by COVID. A lot of students had to begin studying in online sessions. This concerned a lot of these teachers who were worried about parents listening in on their classes. Philadelphia teacher Matthew Kay was one of these teachers.

Kay said on Twitter, "So, this fall, virtual class discussion will have many potential spectators—parents, siblings, etc.—in the same room. We'll never be quite sure who is overhearing the discourse. What does this do for our equity/inclusion work? ... How much have students depended on the (somewhat) secure barriers of our physical classrooms to encourage vulnerability? How many of us have installed some version of 'what happens here stays here' to help this? ... While conversations about race are in my wheelhouse and remain a concern in this no-walls environment, I am most intrigued by the damage that 'helicopter/snowplow' parents can do in the host conversations about gender/sexuality. And while 'conservative' parents are my chief concern—I know that the damage can come from the Left too. If we are engaged in the messy work of destabilizing a kid's racism or homophobia or transphobia—how much do we want their classmates' parents piling on?"[76]

What makes this indoctrination so scary is that these activists are going after kids while they are so young. I have always said, "A child's mind is like wet clay. The younger the child, the wetter the clay." Children are very vulnerable to deception and manipulation, especially when it comes from someone in a position of authority. Millions of kids believe that every year a fat man dressed in red delivers presents to every home in the world. He does this while he drinks Coca-Cola and rides his magic flying reindeer. Why do kids believe this? Because adults tell them it happens. They are that trusting of authority figures. If kids are willing to believe that crazy tale, how hard do you think it will be for a teacher to convince your kids that they are racists? Or that their parents are racists, and they should not talk to them?

A suggestion to counter this indoctrination is for parents to take an active role in their kids' education. Look at the syllabus and course material for every class. At dinner time, talk to your kids about what they learned in school. Be on the lookout for these activists that call themselves teachers. If you think that it is necessary, homeschool your child.

I do want to make something clear. When I suggest solutions, I am not trying to preach or tell people how to raise their kids. There is no one-size-fits-all method when it comes to raising a child. I am just offering advice for anyone who may want it. All I want is for people to be aware of the potential dangers and deal with them accordingly.

Misinformation

Misinformation and indoctrination can go hand in hand. *Irreversible Damage* by Abigail Shrier does a great job of showing this misinformation. Shrier discusses the negative impact that misinformation about gender dysphoria (transgenderism) has on young women. Shrier told the stories of multiple women who "transitioned into men." A common theme that I noticed in *Irreversible Damage* was that schools were often engaged in affirming the gender dysphoria of these young girls. In many cases, the young girl would change her name and preferred pronouns. (Example- a 12-year-old girl named Rebecca wanted to be referred to as "he" and be called "Robert") The school accepted the child's new name and pronoun, and the school did not tell the parents what was going on with their child. A program coordinator for human relations, diversity, and equity of a Los Angeles School District said, "'But schools have expanded to be the hub for a lot more social services and looking more holistically, emotionally, at what's going on with children … Looking at schools as a source of social justice. Our role continues to expand. The outreach is now profound … Yes, we serve the community, but in some places, we have to lead the community'" (*Irreversible Damage*, pg. 60-61). It is not surprising that schools are willing to engage in this kind of activity. But there is another outlet for misinformation that nearly every child has access to.

Social media offers one of the biggest sources of misinformation for kids. Shrier talks about the impact that social media has on kids. There are popular transgender social media influencers who encourage people to transition, even kids. The problem with this is that it can appeal to kids who may not have gender dysphoria. These influencers promote testosterone and breast binding without mentioning the negative side effects. Lastly, some influencers encourage lying to parents in order to transition. Social media also has online forums for transgender people. The problem with these forums is that they are a beacon of conformity. Transgender people who have regrets about transitioning are often blocked from these forums. People who encourage waiting or exercising caution are labeled as bigots. Anyone who speaks against it is quickly excommunicated by their "friends." Shrier wrote about one transgender girl who had a presence in these forums. When this girl was fourteen, she had adult men (identifying as trans women) ask her to "sext" with them. If she refused, she would be accused of shaming them and oppressing these grown men.

This is not just about transgenderism. There are social media influencers who promote terrible behavior. Some of the platforms encourage kids not to take school seriously, be a narcissist, and adopt personality traits that people will not like in the real world. Some social media influencers have pushed forms of underage gambling on kids. Others have posted videos of animal abuse.

There have also been disturbing trends on these platforms. One of these trends involved young people cosplaying as Holocaust victims. Many of these people used makeup to make it seem like they have cuts and bruises. Others used on-screen text to ask questions like "what is your number" and "how did you die". This behavior is disgusting. It is ridiculous for these young people to pretend that they have the slightest idea of the pain the Holocaust victims had to endure. The hardest thing most of those people had to endure is being without the internet for an hour. That is relatively tame, considering Jews had to go days with little to no food. This is insulting the memory of over six million people and is a mockery of one of the worst events in the twentieth century.

In my opinion, the solution to this is not to keep your kids away from the internet altogether. While there may be bad things out there, the internet is filled with fun and information. Take a moderate approach. Let the kids enjoy the benefits of modern technology, but also limit the amount of time children spend on the computer. And don't give a seven-year-old a personal computer or smartphone. Also, focus on communicating effectively with your child. Clearly define good and bad behavior, as well as your expectations. If you instill values into your children, they will not have to learn their values from toxic social media influencers. Lastly, spend time with your kids. Every hour they spend with you is an hour they are not spending in front of a screen.

Pedophilia

Out of everything in this chapter, this one scares me the most. Pedophilia increased over the last couple of years. Fortunately, it is usually shut down once people realize what is going on. I am not worried that pedophilia is going to become mainstream in 2021. I am worried when I ask myself, "Where will we be in five or ten years?"

What really brought this to my attention in 2020 was the movie *Mignonnes*, in English, *Cuties*. The plot involves an African family of immigrants. The protagonist is the family's eleven-year-old daughter Amy. She begins to hang out with a group of girls around the same age. They begin to imitate sexual dances and themes they see on social media. Even though these girls do not understand what it is they are doing, they do it because they believe that they will be popular. As a result of this, Amy begins to change and rebel against her family.

So, what makes this movie so bad? It sexualizes eleven-year-old girls. Some scenes involve the girls dancing in a very sexual manner. In these scenes, the camera zooms in on the girls' buttocks and midsection. Other times the camera focuses on the crotch area. If it sounds disgusting and something that should at the very least concern a lot of people, that's because it is. Film critics did not see it that way. *Cuties* has an 86% critic review score on Rotten Tomatoes.

The fact that this movie was made is not the thing that upsets me the most. What scares me is that people defended this film and dismissed concerns about it. A good example of this is "How 'Cuties' Is Fueling the Far Right's Obsession with Pedophilia," in *Rolling Stone*.[78] The article ignores the people who were concerned about the film. It said that they are overreacting. It references QAnon conspiracy theorists to show that people often accuse the Left of pedophilia. Then it goes on to talk about how Donald Trump and conservatives are mean to Joe Biden. Maybe if it weren't an election year, people would see it differently. This is not just about the movie. As I said, my biggest concern is what happens in the long term. Because pedophiles today are making the same arguments gay rights advocates were making years ago.

In 2018, Mirjam Heine gave a TEDx Talk. She said the following:

According to current research, pedophilia is an unchangeable sexual orientation. Just like, for example, heterosexuality. No one chooses to be a pedophile. No one can cease being one. The difference between pedophilia and other sexual orientations is that living out this sexual orientation will end in a disaster ... It is our responsibility to overcome our negative feelings about pedophiles. And to treat them with the same respect we treat other people with. We should accept that pedophiles are people who have not chosen their sexuality ... We should accept that pedophilia is a sexual preference, a thought, a feeling, and not an act. We should differentiate between child sexual abuse and pedophilia. We shouldn't increase the suffering of pedophiles by excluding them, by blaming and mocking them.[79]

Now I want you, the reader, to do something. I want you to reread that quote but replace the word pedophilia with homosexuality.

It is not just the arguments that are similar. Pedophiles are using similar tactics as well. Leftists like to engage in wordplay. A good example is when NPR talked about how much women spent on tampons. NPR referred to women as "people who menstruate." They did this to market to the transgender community. Pedophiles have tried this type of rebranding. Instead of being called pedophiles, they have referred to themselves as "minor-attracted persons." Pedophiles have also put out their own version of a pride flag.[80] It was not a rainbow flag. It was a flag that had eight lines of colors. It contained two different shades of blue, two different shades of red, two yellow lines, and two white lines. This was likely done to get a place among the LGBTQ community. Fortunately, to their credit, the LGBTQ community adamantly denied the pedophiles' attempt at entry.

I want to make something clear. I am not equating LGBTQ with pedophilia. If there is a rise in pedophilia acceptance, I highly doubt that it will be due to the LGBTQ community. I'm sure most people in the LGBTQ community are good people and believe pedophilia is wrong, for starters. It is safe to assume that they will want nothing to do with something so immoral. Also, there is conflict between groups in the LGBTQ community, so the LGBTQ community probably does not want to add more groups to it. An example of the conflict is that many homosexuals do not believe in gender fluidity. Many believe that men are men, and women are women, and with good reason. If you say that men are women and women are men, then you have essentially destroyed the homosexual identity.

You may be thinking that I am paranoid. But let me ask you something. Ten years ago, would you ever believe that a presidential candidate would suggest that an eight-year-old child should be allowed to choose their gender? A lot of these issues have progressed further than a lot of people ever thought they would. I will leave it to you to decide whether that is good or bad. What concerns me are the leftists in our society. Right now, leftists see LGBTQ members as victims. But what happens when leftists get bored with them? Or what if they decide that there is not any virtue in supporting them anymore? Leftists have gotten somewhat bored with virtue signaling to homosexuals over the last couple of years. They now prefer to pander to trans people. A couple of years ago, I heard how a gay man said he did not buy into gender fluidity. He faced major backlash from leftists who called him transphobic.

I already established that leftists love to virtue signal. They may be willing to embrace anyone who appears to be a victim. The scary thing is not knowing when, if ever, the leftists will draw the line and say enough is enough.

Much like everything else that I mentioned in this chapter, there are no short-term solutions. All we can do is continue to be vigilant about pedophilia. Draw a line in the sand and let leftists know that it will not be crossed. If you see movies or toys that promote pedophilia, speak out. Be willing to boycott companies that go down this path. And watch out for your kids. Because at the end of the day, that's what matters most.

CHAPTER 2

LIBERALS

As I mentioned back in Chapter One, there are differences between a leftist and a liberal. Liberals tend to favor more federal government intervention and approve of American rights and freedoms. Leftists also want a larger government, but it is to a larger degree. It is why there are leftists who consider themselves socialists. Unlike liberals, leftists do not like the freedoms that liberals like. Leftists will push for things such as hate speech laws and laws that allow for discrimination against certain groups. The allowance for discrimination can be seen today in California. California is proposing to repeal Proposition 209. Proposition 209 eliminates affirmative action programs that give "preferential treatment" based on race, sex, color, ethnicity, or national origin. These changes apply to areas such as public employment, public education, and public contracting.

For this chapter, I offer two solutions for change.

1. Side with conservatives
2. Do not automatically see "victims" as virtuous.

Side with Conservatives

I do not envy liberals. Conservatives may face attacks (not literally) from the leftists and liberals. The advantage of this is that the conservatives only need to defend one flank. Think of it as one person coming up to you, grabbing your left arm, and start pulling it in their direction. All you have to do is protect your left side.

It is a different story with liberals and other Left-leaning moderates. These people may agree with some of the policies proposed by leftists. However, they may not wish to see America be torn down. Some liberals may not agree with identity politics. Many liberals still see the value in the freedoms allowed to Americans. These values are things that liberals and conservatives agree on. However, liberals and conservatives usually disagree on what public policy should be implemented.

What you end up with is a game of tug of war between leftists and conservatives, with liberals acting as the rope. Leftists pull liberals to the Left and say, "Come over to our side. You agree with our policy." Conservatives pull to the right and say, "Don't side with them. Their core values are too different from your values." As a result, liberals feel stuck between a rock and a hard place.

One of the reasons that leftists may try to get liberals over to their side is by calling conservatives bigots in one way or another. This is a fallacy. As I noted back in Part 1, leftists claim to be all-loving and inclusive. And they are ... until someone does not think the way a leftist says they should think. Back in Part 1, I used the example of a black conservative. Leftists have no problem labeling them as an Uncle Tom. Another example is the way leftists treated Brandon Straka. Straka created the #WalkAway Campaign. According to walkawaycampaign.com, "The #WalkAway Campaign encourages and supports those on the Left to walk away from the divisive tenets endorsed and mandated by the Democratic Party of today. We are walking away from the lies, the false narratives, the fake news, the race-baiting, the victim narrative, the violence, the vandalism, the vitriol." In September of 2020, the "Walk Away Rescue America" Rally in Dallas was disrupted, and people were assaulted. Straka mentioned that a group of people he was with were chased by leftists and that the leftists threw bottles at them.[90]

The truth is that leftists are some of the biggest bigots out there. They will hate anyone that has a differing opinion from them.

For years, leftists have wildly attacked conservative thought. The best example of this has been on college campuses. I compare these leftist attacks to a wild and rabid dog. Eventually, they will turn around and start attacking the liberals. This is already happening today. It is usually seen when liberals express the importance and value of freedom.

A couple of years ago, Dave Rubin gave a speech at the University of New Hampshire. Rubin calls himself a classical liberal and finds value in the freedoms granted to Americans. Rubin's speech was about the importance of free speech and why everyone should be allowed to express their opinions. Leftists disagreed. There were security threats, and leftists in the audience constantly interrupted Rubin. Fortunately, Rubin was able to get through his speech and Q&A.

A more recent example is a letter to *Harpers Magazine* titled "A Letter on Justice and Open Debate." The letter was signed by many people who are presumably left of center. In fact, there are several things that I politically disagree with. One such instance is the idea that Donald Trump is a major threat to American democracy. But I agree with the thesis of the letter. The letter is firmly against the cancel culture that we have experienced over the last couple of years. The cancel culture seemed to soar in 2020. The letter states that as a society, everyone needs to be able to express themselves freely and openly. If we are to defeat bad ideas, it will be done through open debate and offering better ideas, rather than shaming and repression. One of the best lines of the letter reads as follows:

> We refuse any false choice between justice and freedom, which cannot exist without each other. As writers, we need a culture that leaves us room for experimentation, risk-taking, and even mistakes. We need to preserve the possibility of good-faith disagreement without dire professional consequences. If we won't defend the very thing on which our work depends, we shouldn't expect the public or the state to defend it for us.

A couple of days later, leftists responded to the letter with another letter. *The Objective* published a letter titled "A More Specific Letter on Justice and Open Debate." It was about what you would expect. It was filled with ad hominem fallacies and accusations of dog whistles.

> "The content of the letter also does not deal with the problem of power: who has it and who does not … The writers of the letter use seductive but nebulous concepts and coded language to obscure the actual meaning behind their words in what seems like

an attempt to control and derail the ongoing debate about who gets to have a platform. They are afforded the type of cultural capital from social media that institutions like *Harper's* have traditionally conferred to mostly white, cisgender people."

What the article lacks is any desire or consideration for the freedom of others. This is not shocking. Leftists have no desire for freedom. They see it as a means for someone else to have power or influence. This is a problem because leftists want nearly all the power and influence. What's more, leftists do not aim to achieve power through rational and open debate. They seek to get power through claiming virtue through "speaking for marginalized voices."

In English, "we speak for the victims of our society; therefore, we are right, and you are wrong." This leads me to the second argument.

Do not automatically see "victims" as virtuous

As I noted, leftists tend to care mostly about power. They will say anything and use anyone to get it. Leftists like the idea of "speaking for the marginalized." After all, what could be nobler than standing up for the weak and the oppressed? But what if these people are not being oppressed? Or at least, they are not being oppressed anywhere outside their own mind. What if leftists are using "marginalized people" to give themselves a false moral high ground and grab power?

A recent study by the University of British Columbia[93] showed "individuals with Dark Triad traits—Machiavellianism, Narcissism, Psychopathy—more frequently signal virtuous victimhood, controlling for demographic and socioeconomic variables that are commonly associated with victimization in Western societies."

Below are a couple of important notes from the study.

> Again, we do not doubt that a substantial portion of the victim signals emitted in everyday life convey legitimate victimization experiences of people who would be described by those who know them as virtuous. However, just as there are honorable people who experience misfortune, there are also those who might feign both suffering and virtue to get something they want.

> Virtue signaling is defined as "the conspicuous expression of moral values, done primarily with the intent of enhancing one's standing within a social group" (Oxford English Dictionary). We theorize that three benefits will be accrued from signaling virtue that amplifies the effectiveness of a victim signal. First, by communicating one's superior moral character to the outside world, it can project an image of trustworthiness and allude to the signaler's benevolent intentions of reciprocity … A person who can convincingly present him or herself as virtuous should, on average, be able to induce more people to initiate the voluntary transfer of material or symbolic resources to him or her than someone who sends no signal or who signals that they lack virtue.

> Second, although previous work shows that people are generally trusting (Gilbert, Krull, & Malone, 1990), research also finds that they are motivated to deliberate about and possibly reject the information communicated to them when it carries personal

relevance, which presumably would be the case when they are asked to transfer their resources to a victim signaler (Hasson, Simmons, & Todorov, 2005; Sperber et al., 2010). The close association between honesty and morality (Brambilla, Rusconi, Sacchi, & Cherubini, 2011) suggests that portraying oneself as a moral person can provide supporting evidence for the credibility and legitimacy of one's victim signal.

Third, a virtue signal is also likely to increase observers' perceptions of the signaler's deservingness. A good person who has experienced misfortunes and disadvantages of various kinds is more likely to elicit distress and sympathy from observers, triggering a stronger response to compensate for the undeserved mistreatment (Callan, Dawtry, & Olson, 2012; Callan, Ellard, & Nicol, 2006).[93]

Study 1c "tested whether virtuous victim signals motivate the provision of nontangible support in the form of willingness to do favors for a personally known target. The results support our hypothesis that someone who emits signals of being a virtuous victim is more likely to receive help from others in the form of noneconomic resources."

Study 2b "shows that people who belong to groups that are socially recognized as being part of the victim category (e.g., Haidt, 2016; Jennings, 2015) are more likely to signal victimhood than people who are not in this category, providing evidence for the construct validity of our victim signaling measure."

Study 5 was one of the studies that helped with the main hypothesis. Study 5 showed a positive and significant relationship between virtuous victim signaling and communal narcissism and amoral manipulation, showing that virtuous victim signaling can be used to manipulate others or allow narcissists to fulfill their desire for moral superiority.

Conclusions

In Part 1, I tried to distinguish liberals from leftists because I do not see the two as the same. Leftists push ideas that white supremacists push. The difference is that the hierarchical pyramid is flipped. Liberals should not subjugate themselves to these radicals and their way of thinking.

It goes without saying, if you side against them, they will call you a bigot of some kind, most likely a racist. But the term 'racist' has become so diluted that it does not mean anything. Leftists wield terms like "racist," "bigot," "sexist," and other labels as a club. This club is meant to bash people into silence and submission. They have done it with conservatives, and soon they will start attacking liberals. These people are not on your side. Do not give in to them. Do not give in to their meaningless accusations of bigotry. Do not believe their claims of virtue through victimhood. The truth is that anyone can be a victim if they truly desire to be one.

As I noted before, do not automatically assume that people who claim to be victims are virtuous. They may be trying to emotionally manipulate you into supporting something that you do not want to. Do not let someone else dictate the terms of your life. Hold your ground, stand firm, and most of all, live free.

CHAPTER 3

CORPORATIONS

Have you ever seen the movie *Tropic Thunder*? In the movie, Robert Downey, Jr. and Ben Stiller play actors making a war movie. In one exchange, Stiller is criticized for a recent movie he starred in. The fictional movie was about a mentally disabled man named Simple Jack. *Simple Jack* was universally hated by audiences and film critics. Robert Downey, Jr. tells Ben Stiller that he didn't win any Academy Awards because the Academy does not like it when people play mentally disabled people. Robert Downey, Jr. gives Stiller a final bit of advice and says, "Never go full retard." Here is my advice for corporations today, "Never go full woke."

The biggest reason that a company should "never go full woke" is that woke marketing can backfire harshly. Woke marketing runs the risk of dividing large portions of potential market share. And for what? To appease a handful of people that tweet in all caps for a living. Most people do not like political correctness or cancel culture.

One of the best examples of "going full woke" was the campaign Gillette did in 2019. Gillette ran an ad that was aimed at attacking toxic masculinity. The commercial showed men and boys doing one of two things.

1. Fighting other boys or men
2. Acting sexually aggressive towards women

Keep in mind, Gillette's target demographic is men. Its slogan is "the best a man can get." Clearly the company wanted to send a message to their base. And the message was received. "Don't buy Gillette razors." This may come as a surprise, but men (like everyone else) do not like being talked down to. And so, when Gillette depicted men as hyperaggressive sexual predators, it was not well received. What makes this even more foolish is that they attacked their consumer base. There was nothing to be gained from this. You can't insult a group of people and then expect that group to buy more of your product. Gillette lost about eight billion dollars as a result of this woke marketing.

Companies have tried to pander to the woke crowd multiple times in 2020. Aunt Jemima and Uncle Ben products were canceled. I guess showing fewer black people on products is fighting racism. Remember when Warner Media removed *Gone With the Wind* from HBO Max. *Gone With the Wind* was another victim of cancel culture. Do you know what else was canceled with *Gone With the Wind*? Hattie McDaniel, the first black woman to win an Oscar for her supporting role in the film. The funniest product to be targeted is Mrs. Butterworth syrup. Mrs. Butterworth isn't even black in her current packaging. It's a clear bottle in the shape of a woman. Once the bottle is empty, Mrs. Butterworth is white. But I guess white people are bad, so ...

Do you want another example of going full woke? The 2020 NBA Playoffs. Given the rise of BLM over the summer of 2020, the NBA decided to "go full woke." The league painted "Black Lives Matter" on the courts. Of course, players decided to kneel for the national anthem. But it was different than when Colin Kaepernick knelt in the NFL. This time entire teams were kneeling. And anyone who did not go along with it was mocked. Jonathan Isaac was one of the few players that did not kneel for the national anthem. Soon after, he tore his ACL. It gets worse. An ESPN radio host tweeted out a poll asking, "Is it funny the guy who refused to kneel immediately blew out his knee?"

The players could wear jerseys with political messages on them, "Black Lives Matter," "Equality," "Say Their Names," and "I can't breathe," were a few that were popular. Fans could buy custom NBA jerseys with political messaging on the back of them. Again, you could have "Black Lives Matter" on the jersey. Jerseys could also have "Kill Cops," "Fuck Police," and "Burn Jews," written on the jerseys.[81] Do you know what could not be written on the jerseys? "Free Hong Kong." The NBA wanted to take a stance against the evil American cops who killed fourteen unarmed black people in 2019 (most were justified). But when it comes to speaking out against China (an oppressive autocracy that has put thousands of Muslims into concentration camps and engages in nationwide censorship), the NBA is silent.

"Going full woke" did not do the NBA any favors. The 2020 NBA Finals had the potential to be one of the best NBA Finals ever. It featured the LA Lakers and the Miami Heat. Both teams are popular and are two of the more valuable teams. Forbes lists the Lakers as the second most valuable team in the league, Miami is the twelfth.[82] Both teams have good marketability. Another aspect of the 2020 Finals is that it featured LeBron James trying to win his fourth championship. And he played against a team that he won two NBA titles with. LeBron James is one of the most popular players in the NBA today. I was a fan of his for years. The final piece of the 2020 Finals comes in the form of a tragedy. The iconic Kobe Bryant died in 2020. To say that his team, the Lakers, made the NBA Finals that year is an amazing thing. Fans of Kobe would have loved to watch. The 2020 NBA Finals had enough marketability to set record highs in viewership. Anyone and everyone would have wanted to watch under normal circumstances. Unfortunately, it faced one big problem.

The problem is that fans had enough of the NBA "going full woke." The 2020 NBA Finals was one of the lowest-rated and least viewed finals in NBA Finals history. Every game saw huge losses in ratings and viewership.[83]

Game	2020 (million viewers)	2019 (million viewers)	change
Game 1	7.41	13.51	45.15%
Game 2	6.61	14.05	52.95%
Game 3	5.94	13.44	55.80%
Game 4	7.54	13.16	42.71%
Game 5	8.89	18.34	51.51%
Game 6	8.29	18.34	54.80%

Well, the NBA wants equality, right? I mean, that's what they shoved down the fans' throats. At this rate, the NBA will have equality ... with the WNBA in terms of ratings.

I am not going to say that any company that goes woke is going to lose half of its business. There were several reasons why the NBA had a drop in ratings. Covid-19 delayed the playoffs and pushed it to the fall. Some games were broadcast on the same day as some football or MLB games. Also, fans were not allowed in the arenas, which took a bit of energy out of the game. But social justice still played a significant role in the decline of the NBA. It is why the commissioner of the NBA said that next season there would be a decrease in the social justice messaging on the floor.

All this social justice marketing is not necessary for companies to successfully market their product. You want to shoot a commercial that shows that you think that racism is bad, okay. That's like shooting a commercial that informs people that water is wet. There is nothing special about it. It just makes a couple of narcissists on Twitter feel good about themselves. If you really want to promote your brand, tell the consumer why your product is better than the competition. A couple of years ago, I was looking to buy some orange juice (preferably pulp-free). I came across a jug of Tropicana that was pulp-free, and it claimed it had calcium and vitamin D in it. I bought the juice and found that it tasted pretty damn good. This happened because Tropicana was able to market its product in a way that distinguished itself from others. Not by virtue signaling.

The point I am trying to make to companies is that companies need to stop with this woke pandering. Normal people do not like it. And it is a mistake to try and pander to these leftists because you will never be able to satisfy the woke scolds on Twitter. These are miserable people. They wake up every day trying to find new ways to be a victim. They will always find something to be angry about, even if you give them everything they want. During week one of the NFL, players and coaches kneeled for the national anthem. Some teams stayed in the locker room. The NFL also played "Lift Every Voice and Sing," which has been referred to as the Black national anthem.[84] Teams put statements like "End Racism" in the endzones and on the back of helmets. It is no surprise that this upset fans. What's more, this also failed to please Colin Kaepernick. The former backup quarterback said the NFL is engaging in propaganda. He tweeted, "While the NFL runs propaganda about how they care about Black Life, they are still actively blackballing Eric Reid (@E_Reid35) for fighting for the Black community. Eric set two franchise records last year and is one of the best defensive players in the league."

You can pander all you want. Eventually, the woke mob will come for you. Eventually, you will say something that some hypersensitive leftist will find offensive. And you can't appease your way out of the situation because they will always want more. Stand up to the mob and say no. You will find that a hundred people on Twitter have a lot more bark than bite.

CHAPTER 4

FINAL THOUGHTS

A lot of this book hits on the topic of race relations in America. One of the things that I argue against is this culture of victimhood. It is not wise or productive for someone to see themselves as a victim. It does not matter who you are, what your skin color is, or how much money you have. You are going to fall. You are going to make mistakes. It is on you to pick yourself up and get through the hard times. But if you blame all your mistakes on some invisible oppressor, you deny yourself the ability to grow. I have always said, "The best mistake is the one you never make. The second-best mistake is the one you learn from. The worst mistake is the one you continue to make."

Someone who did not let race hold them back is the late Herman Cain. The businessman and 2012 presidential candidate did not focus on race. He instead focused on hard work, education, and self-improvement. His apathy towards race is demonstrated in this quote.

"I had a college student ask me one time. 'How did you deal with color and race when you were climbing the corporate ladder?' My answer, 'I didn't. Let them deal with it. I didn't focus on that; I didn't have the time.'"[66]

Cain's work towards education and self-improvement can be shown when he worked with the Navy. While he was working for the Navy, Herman Cain was getting outstanding performance reviews. A white co-worker was also getting outstanding marks, but the white co-worker was getting salary increases two months before Cain did. When Cain asked his supervisor about it, he was told it was because the co-worker had a master's degree. When Cain was asked about this in 2020, he said, "I didn't get mad. I went and got me a master's degree."[66]

This is nothing new. Black conservatives have valued self-improvement very highly, and they have fought extremely hard against this victim culture. People like Candace Owens and Larry Elder have opposed it for years. Both have stressed the importance of rebuilding the nuclear family in the black community. Neither one likes the virtue signaling that comes from white guilt. I remember that I saw a video of Candace Owens talking to a white college student. I believe they were talking about the importance of white people acknowledging their privilege. Candace Owens said that it was not important. She said that random white people acknowledging their privilege does not do her any favors. And she said it does not help blacks either.

Candace Owens and Larry Elder are two people that I admire, and I would recommend that people at least listen to the arguments that they make. I would recommend that everyone watch the Larry Elder video where he goes into detail about his father's life and their relationship.[85]

Contrast this with people that talk about how America is racist and filled with white supremacy. Some of the more prominent people include Al Sharpton, Ibram Kendi, and LeBron James. Al Sharpton is considered by many to be one of the biggest political race-baiters of the past thirty years. Ibram Kendi wrote a best-selling book about racism called *How to Be an Antiracist*. LeBron James is a basketball player who said, "A lot of people use this analogy that Black Lives Matter is a movement. It's not a movement. When you're black, it's not a movement. It's a lifestyle. This is a walk of life. I don't like the word 'movement' because unfortunately in America and in society there ain't been no damn movement for us."[86]

I find the quote by LeBron James hilarious. You will see why in a minute. These people are the ones who are yelling from the top of their lungs about how awful America is, and how it is so unfair, and that the deck is stacked so heavily against them. But it did not stop any of them from being successful. A good example is that Ibram Kendi charged a Virginia public school $20,000 for a one-hour Zoom conference on anti-racism. The $20,000 was spent on a forty-five-minute virtual event with Kendi, followed by a fifteen-minute Q&A session. Ibram Kendi made more money in one hour than some people do in six months. Kendi did not even have to leave his house. Hell, he probably didn't even have to wear pants! If he wanted to, he probably could have gotten away with that as long as he did not go full Jeffery Toobin.

It seems that the people who are yelling the loudest are the people who have a lot more than others.

The median American family has a net worth of $97,300 a year. If you separate it by age, you get the following.[87]

Age 35 or younger: $11,100

Age 35-44: $59,800

Age 45-54: $124,200

Age 55-64: $187,300

Age 65-74: $224,100

Age 75 or older: $264,800

Here is the estimated net worth for each of the people listed above.

Al Sharpton- $500,000[88]

Ibram Kendi- estimated to be around $800,000[89]

LeBron James- $480 million[88]

Another evidence that black Americans are not systematically oppressed is that there are whites who pretend to be black. Remember Rachel Dolezal? A couple of years ago, she was a branch president of the NAACP and a civil rights activist. It turns out that she was white and had actively lied about being black.

A more recent example is Jessica Krug. Krug was a professor at George Washington University. She was a historian of Africa and the African diaspora. She made claims of North African Blackness, then U. S.-rooted Blackness, then Caribbean-rooted Bronx Blackness. Like Dolezal, Krug is white.

Why would people pretend to be a part of a group that is "systematically oppressed"? You did not see white people pretending to be black during Jim Crow.

The truth is that these women knew the game. They knew that there was value in being perceived as a victim. Instead of claiming the victimhood of a woman in the patriarchy, they chose to be blacks in a "racist system." As a result, these women were able to gain prominent positions that they probably would not have gotten had they been honest. They wanted to gain victim status to advance themselves. They saw more value in a faux victim status than they saw in their "white privilege." They believed that there was more opportunity for them as blacks than as whites.

But how can someone be a victim and gain exclusive access to professional advancement simultaneously? Maybe it is because blacks are not being systematically oppressed anymore. Maybe at the heart of this country, there is a desire to see everyone succeed. Maybe people like Robin DiAngelo and Ibram Kendi are wrong in their approach.

As I noted back in Part 3, Robin DiAngelo believes that everything is racist, and by acknowledging this, the people can somehow beat racism. This is wrong. For starters, people like DiAngelo call anything and everything racist. It turns out when you do that, people do not take accusations of racism seriously. It's not rocket science; it's a basic rule of economics. If you increase the supply and keep all else constant, you will see the value of something decrease—same idea. If you call everything around you white supremacy, but white supremacy remains an insignificant part of everyday life, people will not put any real value in your accusations. For this reason, I do not buy into DiAngelo's idea of racism and white supremacy. I would compare Robin DiAngelo's version of racism to a hyper-inflated fiat currency. In the same sense that it is everywhere, it is worthless, and nothing good will come from adopting it.

Also, how can someone who believes they are oppressing someone ever see the oppressed as equals? They probably won't. What you will see is people trying to avoid people of other races. Or when those people need to interact, one group is going to be walking on eggshells. Make no mistake; this is just another form of white guilt.

Has America been oppressive in the past? Yes. Does racism still exist today? Yes. Can white guilt be used to beat racism? Absolutely not.

Then how can racism be defeated? It is simple—black excellence. Racists have the idea that blacks are inferior to whites. If you show them that blacks are just as smart, kind, and talented as whites, they lose their core beliefs. Remember Darrell Davis? He was able to get roughly two hundred white supremacists to quit the KKK. He did not get them to walk away by making them feel bad about being racists. Because shockingly, white supremacists do not feel bad about their racism. Through his music and personality, Davis showed them that he did not fit the mold of what they believed a black person was. His excellence as a human being is what shattered the world view of the racists. Not the white fragility nonsense spouted by Robin DiAngelo.

This potential for excellence is within everyone. If you want to beat racism, do not let anyone's potential go to waste. Work hard. Work smart. Do not deny yourself the opportunity to grow.

Remember how Herman Cain did not place value on his race. Instead, he chose to place value in his personal growth and improvement. I told the story of Cain while he was working for the Navy. He worked hard and showed his value to his team. The true dividends of Cain's work showed when he left the Department of the Navy. Cain was given an exit interview. In this interview, the supervisor said something amazing to Cain. The supervisor said, "You know, you have taught me something. I have never worked with a black person before. You taught me don't judge somebody by the color of their skin."[66]

Table 43A

Arrests

by Race and Ethnicity, 2018

[12,212 agencies; 2018 estimated population 247,752,415]

| | Total arrests | | | | | | Percent distribution[1] | | | | | | Total arrests | | | Percent distribution[1] | |
| | Race | | | | | | | | | | | | Ethnicity | | | | |
Offense charged	Total	White	Black or African American	American Indian or Alaska Native	Asian	Native Hawaiian or Other Pacific Islander	Total	White	Black or African American	American Indian or Alaska Native	Asian	Native Hawaiian or Other Pacific Islander	Total[2]	Hispanic or Latino	Not Hispanic or Latino	Total	Hispanic or Latino	Not Hispanic or Latino
TOTAL	7 710 900	5 319 654	2 115 381	164 430	92 737	18 698	100,0	69,0	27,4	2,1	1,2	0,2	6 343 684	1 191 334	5 152 350	100,0	18,8	81,2
Murder and nonnegligent manslaughter	8 957	3 953	4 778	105	94	27	100,0	44,1	53,3	1,2	1,0	0,3	7 050	1 472	5 578	100,0	20,9	79,1
Rape[3]	18 776	12 794	5 376	267	289	50	100,0	68,1	28,6	1,4	1,5	0,3	15 316	4 090	11 226	100,0	26,7	73,3
Robbery	66 789	29 025	36 187	676	641	260	100,0	43,5	54,2	1,0	1,0	0,4	57 048	12 823	44 225	100,0	22,5	77,5
Aggravated assault	298 040	184 527	100 393	6 736	5 078	1 306	100,0	61,9	33,7	2,3	1,7	0,4	254 614	65 056	189 558	100,0	25,6	74,4
Burglary	134 542	91 581	39 617	1 590	1 422	332	100,0	68,1	29,4	1,2	1,1	0,2	114 027	23 200	90 827	100,0	20,3	79,7
Larceny-theft	669 983	448 193	201 086	11 987	7 324	1 393	100,0	66,9	30,0	1,8	1,1	0,2	540 174	78 106	462 068	100,0	14,5	85,5
Motor vehicle theft	69 002	44 512	22 305	1 151	818	216	100,0	64,5	32,3	1,7	1,2	0,3	56 263	14 392	41 871	100,0	25,6	74,4
Arson	6 946	4 938	1 740	137	101	30	100,0	71,1	25,1	2,0	1,5	0,4	5 790	1 055	4 735	100,0	18,2	81,8
Violent crime[4]	392 562	230 299	146 734	7 784	6 102	1 643	100,0	58,7	37,4	2,0	1,6	0,4	334 028	83 441	250 587	100,0	25,0	75,0
Property crime[4]	880 473	589 224	264 748	14 865	9 665	1 971	100,0	66,9	30,1	1,7	1,1	0,2	716 254	116 753	599 501	100,0	16,3	83,7
Other assaults	794 787	512 025	254 360	15 711	10 348	2 343	100,0	64,4	32,0	2,0	1,3	0,3	654 150	125 007	529 143	100,0	19,1	80,9
Forgery and counterfeiting	37 724	25 140	11 637	335	548	64	100,0	66,6	30,8	0,9	1,5	0,2	31 565	5 301	26 264	100,0	16,8	83,2
Fraud	89 610	58 572	28 387	1 419	1 088	144	100,0	65,4	31,7	1,6	1,2	0,2	74 521	9 636	64 885	100,0	12,9	87,1
Embezzlement	11 174	6 923	3 955	122	159	15	100,0	62,0	35,4	1,1	1,4	0,1	9 252	1 193	8 059	100,0	12,9	87,1
Stolen property; buying, receiving, possessir	69 874	44 179	23 661	881	819	334	100,0	63,2	33,9	1,3	1,2	0,5	57 379	11 278	46 101	100,0	19,7	80,3
Vandalism	134 794	91 176	38 887	2 949	1 552	230	100,0	67,6	28,8	2,2	1,2	0,2	112 716	21 479	91 237	100,0	19,1	80,9
Weapons; carrying, possessing, etc.	126 332	68 756	54 715	1 094	1 390	377	100,0	54,4	43,3	0,9	1,1	0,3	100 312	23 663	76 649	100,0	23,6	76,4
Prostitution and commercialized vice	23 502	12 928	9 109	95	1 309	61	100,0	55,0	38,8	0,4	5,6	0,3	21 484	4 379	17 105	100,0	20,4	79,6
Sex offenses (except rape and prostitution)	35 157	25 338	8 403	587	751	78	100,0	72,1	23,9	1,7	2,1	0,2	28 928	7 398	21 530	100,0	25,6	74,4
Drug abuse violations	1 234 178	871 295	333 113	14 148	13 345	2 277	100,0	70,6	27,0	1,1	1,1	0,2	1 044 789	211 692	833 097	100,0	20,3	79,7
Gambling	2 465	1 000	1 198	11	205	51	100,0	40,6	48,6	0,4	8,3	2,1	1 390	341	1 049	100,0	24,5	75,5
Offenses against the family and children	64 357	43 371	18 530	1 895	510	51	100,0	67,4	28,8	2,9	0,8	0,1	51 589	5 999	45 590	100,0	11,6	88,4
Driving under the influence	736 644	597 919	108 703	13 150	14 323	2 549	100,0	81,2	14,8	1,8	1,9	0,3	604 136	147 221	456 915	100,0	24,4	75,6
Liquor laws	128 453	100 687	18 743	6 973	1 876	174	100,0	78,4	14,6	5,4	1,5	0,1	102 624	15 979	86 645	100,0	15,6	84,4
Drunkenness	251 490	193 042	37 781	17 412	2 825	430	100,0	76,8	15,0	6,9	1,1	0,2	233 325	52 491	180 834	100,0	22,5	77,5
Disorderly conduct	248 716	158 533	78 192	9 770	1 926	295	100,0	63,7	31,4	3,9	0,8	0,1	186 261	24 553	161 708	100,0	13,2	86,8
Vagrancy	18 048	12 823	4 458	482	261	24	100,0	71,0	24,7	2,7	1,4	0,1	16 649	2 557	14 092	100,0	15,4	84,6
All other offenses (except traffic)	2 413 408	1 666 825	663 086	54 410	23 550	5 537	100,0	69,1	27,5	2,3	1,0	0,2	1 947 281	317 928	1 629 353	100,0	16,3	83,7
Suspicion	432	237	129	65	1	0	100,0	54,9	29,9	15,0	0,2	0,0	390	15	375	100,0	3,8	96,2
Curfew and loitering law violations	16 720	9 362	6 852	272	184	50	100,0	56,0	41,0	1,6	1,1	0,3	14 661	3 030	11 631	100,0	20,7	79,3

[1] Because of rounding, the percentages may not add to 100.0.

[2] The ethnicity totals are representative of those agencies that provided ethnicity breakdowns. Not all agencies provide ethnicity data; therefore, the race and ethnicity totals will not equal.

[3] The rape figures in this table are aggregate totals of the data submitted based on both the legacy and revised Uniform Crime Reporting definitions.

[4] Violent crimes are offenses of murder and nonnegligent manslaughter, rape, robbery, and aggravated assault. Property crimes are offenses of burglary, larceny-theft, motor vehicle theft, and arson.

Expanded Homicide Data Table 6

Murder

Race, Sex, and Ethnicity of Victim by Race, Sex, and Ethnicity of Offender, 2018
[Single victim/single offender]

Race of victim	Total	Race of offender				Sex of offender			Ethnicity of offender		
		White	Black or African American	Other[1]	Unknown	Male	Female	Unknown	Hispanic or Latino	Not Hispanic or Latino	Unknown
White	3 315	2 677	514	61	63	2 914	383	18	803	1 476	1 036
Black or African American	2 925	234	2 600	17	74	2 603	291	31	83	1 878	964
Other race[1]	220	54	39	122	5	196	22	2	19	132	69
Unknown race	110	46	24	7	33	100	9	1	18	40	52

Sex of victim	Total	Race of offender				Sex of offender			Ethnicity of offender		
		White	Black or African American	Other[1]	Unknown	Male	Female	Unknown	Hispanic or Latino	Not Hispanic or Latino	Unknown
Male	4 639	1 942	2 430	133	134	4 073	521	45	675	2 487	1 477
Female	1 921	1 064	745	72	40	1 731	184	6	245	1 036	640
Unknown sex	10	5	2	2	1	9	0	1	3	3	4

Ethnicity of victim	Total	Race of offender				Sex of offender			Ethnicity of offender		
		White	Black or African American	Other[1]	Unknown	Male	Female	Unknown	Hispanic or Latino	Not Hispanic or Latino	Unknown
Hispanic or Latino	957	772	143	17	25	888	63	6	655	213	89
Not Hispanic or Latino	4 284	1 685	2 357	148	94	3 751	493	40	231	3 193	860
Unknown	1 329	554	677	42	56	1 174	149	6	37	120	1 172

[1] Includes American Indian or Alaska Native, Asian, and Native Hawaiian or Other Pacific Islander.

NOTE: This table is based on incidents where some information about the offender is known by law enforcement; therefore, when the offender age, sex, race, and ethnicity are all reported as unknown, these data are excluded from the table.

REFERENCES

1. "Why I, as a black man, attend KKK rallies. | Daryl Davis | TEDx Naperville." YouTube, TEDx Talks, [video] December 8, 2017. Retrieved from https://www.youtube.com/watch?v=ORp3q1Oaezw

2. "Joe Rogan Experience #1419 - Daryl Davis". YouTube, PowerfulJRE, January 20, 2020. [video] Retrieved from https://www.youtube.com/watch?v=0GTQoWj6yIg

3. "Calling Daryl Davis a Nazi is Woke At Its Worst". YouTube, JRE Clips, February 14, 2020. [video] Retrieved from https://www.youtube.com/watch?v=9J05_5y139I

4. Talcott, S. (September 7, 2019) Antifa calls black man who deradicalizes KKK members a 'white supremacist,' while protesting 'End Racism' event [Online Article]. Retrieved from https://libertyunyielding.com/2019/09/07/antifa-calls-black-man-who-deradicalizes-kkk-members-a-white-supremacist-while-protesting-end-racism-event/

5. "Ben Shapiro speaks at UC Berkeley amid protests." YouTube, Fox News, Sep 15, 2017. [video]Retrieved from https://www.youtube.com/watch?v=0cQEehWcwBc

6. "Outspoken conservative Ben Shapiro says political correctness breeds insanity". YouTube, ABC News, Oct 20, 2017. Retrieved from https://www.youtube.com/watch?v=vj5JXrpwsZs

7. "FULL VIDEO: Hurricane Shapiro Takes Berkeley By Storm". YouTube, The Daily Wire, Sep 15, 2017. [video] Retrieved from https://www.youtube.com/watch?v=aP_9cRUzqMw

8. Chasmar, J. (March 28, 2019) The Economist apologizes for labeling Ben Shapiro 'pop idol of the alt right' [Online Article]. Retrieved from https://www.washingtontimes.com/news/2019/mar/28/economist-apologizes-labeling-ben-shapiro-pop-idol/

9. "What Defunding the Police Really Means". blacklivesmatter.com. July 6, 2020 [video] https://blacklivesmatter.com/what-defunding-the-police-really-means/

10. Black Lives Matter Website (no publication date) What We Believe [Website] Retrieved from https://blacklivesmatter.com/what-we-believe/ Other referenced areas from website https://blacklivesmatter.com/about/ https://blacklivesmatter.com/six-years-strong/ https://blacklivesmatter.com/herstory/

    https://www.blacklivesmatterchicago.com/about-us/
    https://blacklivesmatterboston.org/philosophy
    https://blacklivesmatterboston.org/about
    http://www.blacklivesmatterdmv.org/about/
    https://www.blacklivesmatterchicago.com/nocopacademy/

11. Washington Post detailed police shootings https://github.com/washingtonpost/data-police-shootings/blob/master/fatal-police-shootings-data.csv

12. Washington Post (updated June 25, 2020) Fatal Force [website] Retrieved from https://www.washingtonpost.com/graphics/2019/national/police-shootings-2019/ (Note. Website was updated on July 1, 2020. Number of deaths increased from 999 to 1017. Information used was from June 25, 2020 because I could not sort or filter the new information, this can add a small margin of error to the percentages. new information retrieved from https://www.washingtonpost.com/graphics/investigations/police-shootings-database/)

13. FBI (no release date) Murder: Race, Sex, and Ethnicity of Victim by Race, Sex, and Ethnicity of Offender, 2018 [online table] Retrieved from https://ucr.fbi.gov/crime-in-the-u.s/2018/crime-in-the-u.s.-2018/tables/expanded-homicide-data-table-6.xls

14. Washington Post (no release date) About this story. [Online] Retrieved from https://github.com/washingtonpost/data-police-shootings

15. Houmard, C. (February 14, 2020) Temple cop charged with manslaughter in shooting death of Michael Dean. [Online Article] https://www.kcentv.com/article/news/local/temple-officer-charged-with-manslaughter-in-michael-dean-death/500-e304f89f-f5df-48ff-ba2c-4adf8ae86746

16. Ortiz, E. (December 20, 2019) Fort Worth police officer who fatally shot Atatiana Jefferson indicted on murder charge [Online Article] https://www.nbcnews.com/news/us-news/fort-worth-police-officer-who-fatally-shot-atatiana-jefferson-indicted-n1105916

17. Wallace, S. (June 24, 2019) 'I Could've Been Dead': Newark Police Officer Indicted in Deadly Traffic Stop Shooting Speaks Out in I-Team Exclusive. [Online Article] https://www.nbcnewyork.com/news/local/police-officer-manslaughter-arrest-jovanny-crespo-interview-newark-new-jersey-body-cam-shooting-death-video/1639787/

18. FBI (No release date) Arrests by Race and Ethnicity, 2018. [Online Police data] Retrieved from https://ucr.fbi.gov/crime-in-the-u.s/2018/crime-in-the-u.s.-2018/tables/table-43

19. DOJ (March 4, 2015) DEPARTMENT OF JUSTICE REPORT REGARDING THE CRIMINAL INVESTIGATION INTO THE SHOOTING DEATH OF MICHAEL BROWN BY FERGUSON, MISSOURI POLICE OFFICER DARREN WILSON. [Online document] Retrieved from https://www.justice.gov/sites/default/files/opa/press-releases/attachments/2015/03/04/doj_report_on_shooting_of_michael_brown_1.pdf

20. Cwik, C. (June 3, 2020) Drew Brees addresses NFL players kneeling in 2020: 'I will never agree with anybody disrespecting the flag' [Online Article] Retrieved from https://sports.yahoo.com/drew-brees-addresses-nfl-players-kneeling-in-2020-i-will-never-agree-with-anybody-disrespecting-the-flag-164423496.html

21. Morse, B. (June 4, 2020) Drew Brees issues apology for 'insensitive' comments. [Online article] Retrieved from https://www.cnn.com/2020/06/04/sport/drew-brees-apology-nfl-spt-intl/index.html

22. Scott, N. (June 4, 2020) Drew Brees posts lengthy apology over protest comments: 'I should do less talking and more listening' [Online Article] Retrieved from https://ftw.usatoday.com/2020/06/drew-brees-apology-protest

23. [Online Dictionary] Retrieved from https://dictionary.cambridge.org/us/dictionary/english/wokeness

24. Wallace, D. (June 24, 2020) White DC protester seen yelling in faces of black cops in viral video: 'They're a part of the problem' [Online Article] Retrieved from https://www.foxnews.com/us/dc-white-protester-yell-face-black-police-officers-part-of-problem

25. Golden, C. (July 7, 2020) 'It Makes People Cry': Watch NYC Official's Insane Rant After White Colleague Holds Black Baby on Lap. Retrieved From https://www.westernjournal.com/makes-people-cry-watch-nyc-officials-insane-rant-white-colleague-holds-black-baby-lap/

26. Gesualdi-Gilmore, L. (July 16, 2020) 'DEEPLY INSULTING' African American museum accused of 'racism' over whiteness chart linking hard work and nuclear family to white culture. Retrieved from https://www.the-sun.com/news/1149007/african-american-museum-whiteness-chart-protestant-values/

27. District Herald (May 31, 2020) You Love To See It: Rich Writer Cheers Rioters Burning Poor Areas, Calls Them 'Animals' When They Get To His. Retrieved from https://districtherald.com/you-love-to-see-it-rich-writer-cheers-rioters-burning-poor-areas-calls-them-animals-when-they-get-to-his/

28. Mansfield, M. (July 1, 2020) 'THIS IS MY PARK' Black man who rips down BLM signs is assaulted by a white man who yells at him to 'go home, bro'. https://www.the-sun.com/news/1070869/black-man-rips-blm-posters-assault-white-man/

29. Bleiweis, R. (March 24, 2020) "Quick Facts About the Gender Wage Gap" [Online Article] Retrieved from https://www.americanprogress.org/issues/women/reports/2020/03/24/482141/quick-facts-gender-wage-gap/

30. Mac Donald, Heather (published in 2016) The War On Cops How the New Attack On Law and Order Makes Everyone Less Safe. Published by Encounter Books

31. Bacon, J. (June 26, 2017) "Philando Castile's family settles lawsuit with city for $3 million" [Online Article] Retrieved from https://www.usatoday.com/story/news/nation/2017/06/26/philando-castiles-family-settles-suit-city-3-m/427872001/

32. Dorn, S. (July 4, 2020) "Shootings soar 205 percent after NYPD disbands anti-crime unit" [Online Article] Retrieved from https://nypost.com/2020/07/04/shootings-soar-205-percent-after-nypd-disbands-anti-crime-unit/

33. NYPD (July 6, 2020) "NYPD Announces Citywide Crime Statistics for June 2020" [Online Statistics] Retrieved from https://www1.nyc.gov/site/nypd/news/pr0706/nypd-citywide-crime-statistics-june-2020

34. Nolte, J. (July 15, 2020) "Nolte: Black Activists in New York City Want Their Police Back" [Online Article] Retrieved from https://www.breitbart.com/politics/2020/07/15/nolte-black-activists-in-new-york-city-want-their-police-back/

35. Kissiah, M. (April 30, 2020) "List of Police Officer Equipment and Accessories" [Online Article] Retrieved from https://www.einvestigator.com/police-officer-equipment/

36. U.S. Equal Employment Opportunity Commission (Dec 12, 2016) "Depression, PTSD, & Other Mental Health Conditions in the Workplace: Your Legal Rights." [Online Article] https://www.eeoc.gov/laws/guidance/depression-ptsd-other-mental-health-conditions-workplace-your-legal-rights

37. Burnley, A. (June 26, 2017) "Former Washington Middle School students speak out about rough days there" [Online Article] Retrieved from https://www.wearegreenbay.com/news/local-news/former-washington-middle-school-students-speak-out-about-rough-days-there/

38. Award-winning teacher Kerstin Westcott resignation speech in Green Bay School. YouTube, Cringe Panda. (Jul 10, 2017) https://www.youtube.com/watch?v=-SRCY8FqoyQ

39. Obama: Involved dads could curb violence. Youtube, CNN (Feb 15, 2013) [video] https://www.youtube.com/watch?v=IwLq_KKHJXg

40. Pew Research Center. (June 27, 2016) "On views of Race and Inequality, Blacks and Whites Are Worlds Apart." [Online Statistics] Retrieved from https://www.pewsocialtrends.org/2016/06/27/1-demographic-trends-and-economic-well-being/

41. Fagan, P. (March 17, 1995) The Real Root Causes of Violent Crime: The Breakdown of Marriage, Family, and Community. [Online Article] Retrieved from https://www.heritage.org/crime-and-justice/report/the-real-root-causes-violent-crime-the-breakdown-marriage-family-and#:~:text=State%2Dby%2Dstate%20analysis%20by,of%20families%20abandoned%20by%20fathers.

42. Black Fathers Matter YouTube. PragerU. (Jun 13, 2016) [video] https://www.youtube.com/watch?v=FszQelEQ2KY

43. Kruse, B. (June 22, 2020) CHOP: Seattle mayor walks back 'summer of love' comment [Online article] Retrieved from https://www.q13fox.com/news/chop-seattle-mayor-walks-back-summer-of-love-comment

44. Ramirez, Q. (June 24, 2020) Capitol Hill businesses file lawsuit against city for handling of 'CHOP' [Online Article] Retrieved from https://komonews.com/news/local/capitol-hill-businesses-file-lawsuit-against-city-for-handling-of-chop

45. Ruiz, Michael. (June 24, 2020) Seattle's CHOP has seen shootings, vandalism, other crimes as officials vow to dismantle it. [Online Article] Retrieved from https://www.foxnews.com/us/seattles-chop-has-seen-shootings-vandalism-other-crimes-as-officials-vow-to-dismantle-it

46. Brownstone, S. (June 30, 2020) Shooting at Seattle's CHOP protest site kills 16-year-old boy, leaves 14-year-old seriously injured. Retrieved from https://www.seattletimes.com/seattle-news/crime/shooting-at-seattles-chop-protest-site-leaves-2-in-critical-condition/

47. KIRO 7 news staff. (July 1, 2020) Seattle police, city workers clear CHOP after mayor issues emergency order Retrieved from https://www.kiro7.com/news/local/seattle-police-clearing-chop-after-mayor-issues-emergency-order/RBYYWMGLRRHKXOQM3GENBCVNBA/

48. KING 5 staff. (June 28, 2020) Protesters march to Seattle Mayor Durkan's house as 'CHOP' scene continues Retrieved from https://www.king5.com/article/news/local/protests/seattle-city-councilmember-kshama-sawant-joined-a-large-group-of-protesters-outside-the-chop-zone-who-marched-to-durkans-house-on-sunday-afternoon/281-b8177945-8696-4cfb-afa8-dfda5f9ccf1f

49. Steele, Shelby. (published in 2006) White Guilt How Blacks and Whites Together Destroyed the Promise of the Civil Rights Era. [Book] Published by HarperCollins Publisher

50. Justice, T. (August 6,2020) Gallup: 81 Percent Of Black Americans Want Police Protection, Some Want More. [online article] Retrieved from https://thefederalist.com/2020/08/06/gallup-81-percent-of-black-americans-want-police-protection-some-want-more/

51. Saad, L. (August 5, 2020) Black Americans Want Police to Retain Local Presence [online article] Retrieved from https://news.gallup.com/poll/316571/black-americans-police-retain-local-presence.aspx

52. NYPD. (August 3, 2020) NYPD Announces Citywide Crime Statistics for July 2020. [online article] Retrieved from https://www1.nyc.gov/site/nypd/news/p0803a/nypd-citywide-crime-statistics-july-2020

53. Marsh, J. (August 3, 2020) de Blasio admits city skipped permit process to paint Black Lives Matter murals. [online article] Retrieved from https://nypost.com/2020/08/03/de-blasio-admits-city-skipped-permit-process-to-paint-blm-murals/

54. Culver, J. (July 14, 2020) 1-year-old killed at New York City cookout shooting, three injured. [online article] Retrieved from https://www.usatoday.com/story/news/nation/2020/07/14/nyc-cookout-shooting-leaves-1-year-old-dead-3-injured/5432785002/

55. Isabel V. Sawhill and Ron Haskins. (September 1, 2003) Work and Marriage: The Way to End Poverty and Welfare. [online] Retrieved from https://www.brookings.edu/research/work-and-marriage-the-way-to-end-poverty-and-welfare/

56. WWL Staff. (June 3, 2020) Drew Brees' comments blasted by teammates: 'You're part of the problem' [Online Article] Retrieved by https://www.wwltv.com/article/sports/nfl/saints/drew-brees-blasted-by-teammates-youre-part-of-the-problem/289-6ccfcf49-6fff-44e6-8c74-c93ecba4b4b5

57. Forbes. (no date) Sports Money: 2020 NFL Valuations [Online Article] https://www.forbes.com/nfl-valuations/list/#tab:overall

58. Bialik, K. (February 8, 2019) For the fifth time in a row, the new Congress is the most racially and ethnically diverse ever [Online Article] https://www.pewresearch.org/fact-tank/2019/02/08/for-the-fifth-time-in-a-row-the-new-congress-is-the-most-racially-and-ethnically-diverse-ever/

59. Box office Mojo Top Lifetime Grosses [Online List] https://www.boxofficemojo.com/chart/top_lifetime_gross/?area=XWW (DiAngelo's source)

60. Garcia, A. (May 16, 2018) Carolina Panthers sold to hedge fund founder [Online Article] https://money.cnn.com/2018/05/16/news/companies/panthers-carolina-nfl-sold-david-tepper/index.html

61. Stossel: Saving Kids From Government Schools. YouTube. ReasonTV (Jan 23, 2018) [video] https://www.youtube.com/watch?v=QS2AcuhFdhQ

62. DiAngelo, R. and Schroeder, C. (2010) Addressing Whiteness in Nursing Education The Sociopolitical

Climate Project at the University of Washington School of Nursing. [Online Article] https://robindiangelo.com/wp-content/uploads/2016/01/SchroederDiAngelo-1.pdf

63. CDC. (last updated September 10, 2020) Infant Mortality. [Online article] https://www.cdc.gov/reproductivehealth/maternalinfanthealth/infantmortality.htm#:~:text=In%20 2018%2C%20infant%20mortality%20rates,American%20 Indian%2FAlaska%20Native%3A%208.2

64. FBI. (May 4, 2020) FBI Releases 2019 Statistics on Law Enforcement Officers Killed in the Line of Duty. [Online article] https://www.fbi.gov/news/pressrel/press-releases/fbi-releases-2019-statistics-on-law-enforcement-officers-killed-in-the-line-of-duty#:~:text=According%20to%20 statistics%20reported%20to,41%20officers%20died%20 in%20accidents.

65. National Consortium for the Study of Terrorism and Responses to Terrorism. (last update unknown) The Global Terrorism Database. [Online database] START weblink- https://www.start.umd.edu/data-and-tools/start-datasets GTD weblink- https://www.start.umd.edu/gtd/

66. Elder, Larry. Uncle Tom. Uncletom.com, June 19, 2020. [Documentary] https://www.uncletom.com/

67. McClallan, Scott. (July 6, 2020) Gov. Walz requests federal funding after riots caused $500 million in damage. [Online Article] Retrieved from- https://www. thecentersquare.com/minnesota/gov-walz-requests-federal-funding-after-riots-caused-500-million-in-

damage/article_bcf0f4d4-bfaf-11ea-abc6-b77194d7f388.
html#:~:text=Rioters%20burned%2C%20looted%20or%20
vandalized,police%20beating%20of%20Rodney%20King

68. Feuerherd, Ben. (June 26, 2020) Minneapolis City
Council approves measure to abolish police force [Online
Article] Retrieved from https://nypost.com/2020/06/26/
minneapolis-city-council-approves-measure-to-abolish-
police-force/

69. Schwarts, Ian. (June 8, 2020) Minneapolis City Council
President On Dismantling Police: Wanting To Call The
Police "Comes From A Place Of Privilege". Retrieved from
https://www.realclearpolitics.com/video/2020/06/08/
minneapolis_city_council_president_on_dismantling_
police_wanting_to_call_the_police_comes_from_a_place_
of_privilege.html

70. Linge, Mary. (June 27, 2020) Minneapolis council
members who voted to abolish cops get private security.
[Online Article] Retrieved from https://nypost.
com/2020/06/27/minneapolis-council-members-who-
voted-to-abolish-cops-get-private-security/

71. Jewers, Chris and Zilber, Ariel. (September 17, 2020)
'Residents say police are nowhere to be seen': 'Alarmed'
Minneapolis City Council demands answers from its
police chief over 15 percent rise in violent crime - two
months after slashing his budget by $1m. [Online Article]
Retrieved from https://www.dailymail.co.uk/news/
article-8743923/Minneapolis-City-Council-alarmed-surge-
violent-crime-two-months-cutting-police-budget.html

72. Brown, Jon (August 2, 2020) 'Do As They Say': Minneapolis Police Tell Residents To 'Be Prepared To Give Up' Personal Belongings To Robbers. [Online Article] Retrieved from https://www.dailywire.com/news/do-as-they-say-minneapolis-police-tell-residents-to-be-prepared-to-give-up-personal-belongings-to-robbers

73. The Guardian (No date) Nearly two-thirds of US young adults unaware 6m Jews killed in the Holocaust. [Online Article] Retrieved from https://www.theguardian.com/world/2020/sep/16/holocaust-us-adults-study

74. BLM At School (No date) The Demands. [Web Site]. Retrieved From https://www.blacklivesmatteratschool.com/the-demands.html

75. "Young Americans Know Nothing About The 4th of July." YouTube, Campus Reform. [video] Jul 2, 2020. Retrieved from https://www.youtube.com/watch?v=YC4Qg4IUkvY

76. Colton, Emma. (August 10, 2020) Philadelphia public school teacher worries about 'conservative' parents listening in on virtual classes. [Online Article] Retrieved From https://www.washingtonexaminer.com/news/philadelphia-public-school-teacher-worries-about-conservative-parents-listening-in-on-virtual-classes#:~:text=Matthew%20Kay%2C%20who%20teaches%20English,sexuality%2C%20the%20Daily%20Wire%20reported.

77. Shrier, Abigail. (Published in 2020) Irreversible Damage The Transgender Craze Seducing Our Daughter. [Book] Published by Regnery Publishing

78. Dickson, EJ. (September 14, 2020) How 'Cuties' Is Fueling the Far Right's Obsession With Pedophilia. [Online Article] Retrieved from https://www.rollingstone.com/culture/culture-commentary/cuties-netflix-far-right-controversy-pedophilia-1057736/

79. Staff Writer. (June 22, 2018) TEDx speaker says, 'pedophilia is a natural sexual orientation.' [Online Article] Retrieved from http://caldronpool.com/tedx-speaker-says-pedophilia-is-a-natural-sexual-orientation/ Note* with this source, I reference a video that confirms the transcript "You Won't Believe This Sick Ted Talk." YouTube. DailyWire, (Jun 24, 2019) Retrieved from https://www.youtube.com/watch?v=SEW3hjdIjaE

80. Coates, Erin. (July 10, 2018) Pedophiles Desperately Trying To Join LGBT Movement with Their Own 'Acceptance' Flag. [Online Article] Retrieved from https://www.westernjournal.com/pedophiles-desperately-join-lgbt-movement-acceptance-flag/

81. Gottschalk, Jonah. (July 13, 2020) NBA Bans Custom Jerseys With 'FreeHongKong,' But Allows 'Burn Jews' And 'KillCops.' [Online Article] Retrieved from https://thefederalist.com/2020/07/13/nba-bans-custom-jerseys-with-freehongkong-but-allows-burn-jews-and-kill-cops/

82. Forbes. (No Date) The Business Of Basketball. [Online Article]Retrieved from https://www.forbes.com/nba-valuations/list/#tab:overall

83. Glaspiegal, Ryan. (October 13, 2020) NBA Finals Ratings Were Officially the Lowest in Modern History. [Online Article] Retrieved from https://www.outkick.com/nba-finals-ratings-were-officially-the-lowest-in-modern-history/

84. The Guardian. (September 13, 2020) Colin Kaepernick attacks NFL 'propaganda' as teams protest on opening weekend. [Online Article] Retrieved from https://www.theguardian.com/sport/2020/sep/13/nfl-teams-kneel-stay-in-locker-rooms-anthem-protests

85. Larry Elder on Hating & Reconciling w/ His Father; Black Men Being Crushed By Excuses NOT 'Racism'. YouTube. BOND: Rebuilding the Man [video] July 15, 2016 Retrieved from https://www.youtube.com/watch?v=QorhoRWNFK8

86. OmniSport. (July 24, 2020) LeBron James says Black Lives Matter isn't a movement: 'It's a lifestyle'. [Online Article] Retrieved from https://www.sportingnews.com/us/nba/news/lebron-james-black-lives-matter-movement-lifestyle/mzhikjxncj431rrjfholkmovk

87. Elkins, Kathleen. (October 13, 2020) Here's the net worth of the average American family. [Online Article] Retrieved from https://www.cnbc.com/2019/05/14/the-net-worth-of-the-average-american-family.html

88. Celebrity Net Worth. (no author or date) [Online Articles] LeBron James Retrieved from https://www.celebritynetworth.com/richest-athletes/nba/lebron-james-net-worth/

Al Sharpton retrieved from https://www.celebritynetworth.com/richest-politicians/al-sharpton-net-worth/#:~:text=Al%20Sharpton%20Net%20Worth%20and,prejudice%20and%20injustice%20in%20America.

89. (September 28, 2020) Ibram X. Kendi Net Worth, Wife, Wiki, Bio, Age, Height, Family. [Online Article] Retrieved from https://www.wikifyindia.com/ibram-x-kendi/

90. Cheong, Ian. (September 5, 2020) BREAKING: BLM mob violently attacks Trump supporters in Dallas. [Online Article]. Retrieved from https://thepostmillennial.com/breaking-blm-radical-attacks-stage-at-pro-trump-walkaway-rally-security-guard-who-stopped-him-detained-by-police

91. Harpers Magazine. (July 7, 2020) A Letter on Justice and Open Debate. [Online Article] Retrieved From https://harpers.org/a-letter-on-justice-and-open-debate/

92. The Objective. (July 10, 2020) A More Specific Letter on Justice and Open Debate. [Online Article] Retrieved from https://theobjective.substack.com/p/a-more-specific-letter-on-justice

93. Ok, E., Yi Qian, Strejcek, Brendan, and Aquino, Karl. (May 1, 2020) Signaling Virtuous Victimhood as Indicators of Dark Triad Personalities. [Research Paper] Retrieved from https://www.gwern.net/docs/psychology/2020-ok.pdf

94. Fitzsimmons, Emma. (September 30, 2020) Progressives Defeat Brooklyn Project That Promised 20,000 Jobs.

[Online Article] Retrieved from https://www.nytimes.com/2020/09/23/nyregion/industry-city-rezoning-nyc.html

95. Saavedra, Ryan. (October 28, 2020) Chick-Fil-A Went Woke Earlier This Year Amid Riots. That Didn't Stop Looters From Hitting Their Store In Philadelphia. [Online Article] Retrieved From https://www.dailywire.com/news/chick-fil-a-went-woke-earlier-this-year-amid-riots-that-didnt-stop-looters-from-hitting-their-store-in-philadelphia

96. Mastrangelo, Alana. (October 24, 2020) Chelsea Handler: I Had to Remind 50 Cent He's Black After His Trump Support. [Online Article] Retrieved from https://www.breitbart.com/entertainment/2020/10/24/chelsea-handler-i-had-to-remind-50-cent-hes-black-after-his-trump-support/

97. DiAngelo, Robin. (written in 2018) White Fragility [Book] Published by Beacon Press

98. Civiqs.com. (Last updated November 8, 2020) Do you support or oppose the Black Lives Matter movement? (Online Poll) Retrieved from https://civiqs.com/results/black_lives_matter?annotations=true&uncertainty=true&zoomIn=true

99. (performed May 26, 2020) Hennepin County Medical Examiner's Office Autopsy Report [Autopsy Report] Retrieved from http://www.autopsyfiles.org/reports/Other/floyd,%20george_report.pdf

100. Sutter, Mark E. MD, Gerona, Roy R., Ph.D., Davis, M. Thais, MD, et al. (January 2017) Fatal Fentanyl: One Pill Can Kill. [Online Report] Retrieved from http://uthscsa.edu/artt/AddictionJC/2020-02-11-Sutter.pdf

101. The Associated Press (July 9, 2020) George Floyd transcript: Read it in full here [Online Article] Retrieved from https://www.twincities.com/2020/07/09/george-floyd-transcript-read-it-in-full-here/

102. Gordon, James (August 11, 2020) Full uncensored footage of George Floyd's arrest, including his harrowing final moments as an officer knelt on his neck are revealed in 30-minute-long police bodycam video. [Online Article and Video] Retrieved from https://www.dailymail.co.uk/news/article-8614589/First-length-bodycam-footage-shows-George-Floyds-harrowing-final-moments-brutal-arrest.html

103. "What Defunding the Police Really Means." Blacklivesmatter.com, [video] July 6, 2020. Retrieved from https://blacklivesmatter.com/what-defunding-the-police-really-means/

9 781736 734247